A Centenary Commemoration

North Sea Incident

Assault on the Hull fishing fleet 21-22 October 1904
and
the origins and fate of the box fleet.

by

Arthur G. Credland

NORTH SEA INCIDENT

British Library Cataloguing in Publication Data.
A catalogue record for this book is available from the British Library.

First published 2004

© 2004 Arthur Credland

Published by Hull Museums and Galleries

ISBN 0 904490 32 7

'For online details of the North Sea Incident visit www.hullmaritime.com'

NORTH SEA INCIDENT

October 21-22 1904

Acknowledgements

My thanks to all those who have helped make this publication possible. The support of Brian Hayton, Head of Museum Services, and contributions from my colleagues Craig Barclay and Clare Parsons are much appreciated.

No local historian would be able to work effectively without the enthusiasm and willing help of the Hull Library Services and Archives- namely, David Smith and his colleagues in the Local Studies department, Jenny Newby and the staff of the Reference Library and Martin Taylor and his associates in the Hull City Record Office. In addition, Alec Gill, Mike Thompson and Robert Wise have all helped to clarify details of the vessels involved in the North Sea Incident. Chris Ketchell and the Local History Unit over a number of years have contributed useful nuggets of information to add to the story. Silas Taylor of AMJ Solicitors (Andrew M. Jackson represented the trawler owners at the Board of Trade inquiry) generously lent scrapbooks and copies of the official government reports, which have been preserved in their office archives. In addition, Fred Lake kindly arranged for copies to be made of the material in the Admiralty Library.

The typescript was prepared, from my notorious scribblings, by Lisa Stokes and the final production superintended by Steve Tongue in Hull Print with layout and design work by Hull Design.

Arthur Credland, Hull Maritime Museum.

CONTENTS

NOTE

At the time of the incident, Russia was still using the Julian calendar, which was 13 days behind the Gregorian calendar; hence, according to the Imperial Fleet, the encounter took place 8-9 October. Unless otherwise stated all dates have been converted to New Style.

The transliteration of Russian names has varied considerably over time. When quoting from original documents the early forms have been retained, otherwise the most generally used version has been chosen.

Hark to the mourners' weeping,
Sobb'd with 'bated breath.
Whilst in anguish keeping,
Watch o'er those whose death
Came while perils scorning
On the mighty deep—
Night—o'er shadow'd morning,
Marshalling death's long sleep.

List to the indignation,
From men of every tongue;
The mighty British nation,
Whose heart's deep chords are wrung.
Hark to the children's crying,
List to the widow's prayers.
Daughter of Fair Britannia,
A Nation's grief is theirs,

God His watch is keeping,
O'er the children's tears,
Daughters of Fair Britannia,
Calm with love their fears.
Help the lonely widow
To lock within the breast,
Her sorrow and her anguish,
Remembering—God knows best.
—REGINALD T. SHUTTE.

1 Attacked on the North Sea

A postcard showing the Gamecock fleet under attack.

The 'North Sea Incident' of the 21-22 October, when the Hull fishing fleet was attacked by Russian warships, is now part of Hull's 'folk memory'. A physical reminder of the incident is the fishermen's monument on the Hessle Road and, more dramatically, the shell-torn head of the companionway of the trawler *Mino* displayed in the Hull Maritime Museum. After the lapse of a hundred years, the affair seems not only tragic but scarcely credible.

For a city which has become accustomed to disasters involving her fishermen, the bombardment of the Hull trawlers, with the ensuing loss of the *Crane*, still remains a startling event. The number of men lost was small, two were killed outright and a third died some while later of the after-effects, but the nature of the assault is peculiarly shocking, a totally unprovoked attack by a 'friendly' nation and the apparent lack of concern for casualties by the Russian command.

The incident was a totally unexpected and unpredictable result, in European waters, of the struggle between two imperialist states, Russia and Japan, trying to establish and extend their power and influence thousands of miles away in the Far East. Outside of Hull the story is largely forgotten and often does not even rate a footnote in the histories of the twentieth century. Its memory has been all but obliterated by the horror and carnage of the Great War, which began only a decade later and itself an outcome, inevitable as it now appears to us, of the web of alliances between the European imperial powers.

Immediately after the sinking of the *Crane* there was even the possibility of some sort of punitive

A skipper protecting a cabin boy; artist's impression from The Graphic.

attack by Britain or an attempt to 'arrest' the Russian Baltic fleet during its long journey to engage the Japanese. The apologies of the Russian government and the award of compensation following the tribunal in Paris defused a tense situation. Britain in the meantime had held her hand, fearful of destabilising even more a failing Russian state beset by political assassinations and the rumblings of revolution. The annihilation of the Russian navy at Tsushima in 1905 was popularly regarded as a just punishment, and the need for further threats or pressure by Britain and her allies no longer seemed relevant.

The continuing weakness and incompetence of the Tsarist regime reached a crisis with the mismanagement of the armed forces in the Great War, which led to the abdication of the Tsar in 1917 and the Bolshevik revolution. The communist state which followed has, in its turn, fallen and the former U.S.S.R. struggles to establish a modern democracy after a long history of autocracy and dictatorship.

In St Petersburg (Petrograd, Leningrad) the last survivor of the Baltic fleet, the cruiser *Aurora*, is preserved as a proud symbol of Russia in the twentieth century. A shot fired from the forward gun signalled the attack on the Winter Palace at the beginning of the October Revolution. It is also a reminder of a tragedy in the North Sea and the unexpected outcomes of imperial ambition.

The purpose of the following text is to relate the events in the North Sea and their aftermath. It will attempt to explain how and why the Russian fleet could even imagine they were under threat from the Japanese, with whom they were then at war, when the nearest enemy bases were some 18,000 miles away. [1]

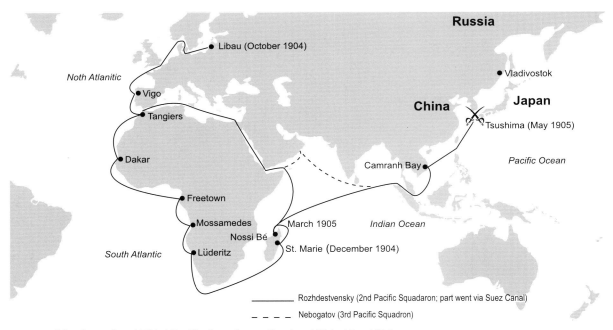

Routes of the Second and Third Pacific Squadrons, October 1904 - May 1905.

The North Sea Incident

The first news of the attack on the Hull fishing fleet [2] was made public at 7pm on the evening of Sunday 23rd October, when announcements were posted up in the offices of the *Hull Daily Mail.*

The trawler *Moulmein* had arrived with the bodies of Skipper Smith of the *Crane* and the third hand W. R. Leggett, both men killed by gun-fire on the North Sea. A special morning edition was rushed out on Monday, and the evening edition relates the as yet sketchy details[3] but a more circumstantial account relating the eyewitness evidence of Captain Peaker of the *Magpie* is reprinted from the London *Daily Mail:*

"The fish carrier *Magpie* arrived in the Thames last night, and berthed at the wharf of her

Illustration from The Graphic, 29 October 1904, entitled 'The first shot: the scene on the trawler Mino, from information supplied by the latter's engineer, James Tubb'.

Russian Outrage on the Dogger Bank, October 1904; photograph of an original painting, now lost, by John Skelly.

Field-glasses said to have belonged to Skipper Smith of the Crane (Hull Maritime Museum)

Built in 1903 there are no known photographs of the Crane (H246). This is a posthumous 'portrait' of the vessel, signed and dated 1904, by the marine artist E.K. Redmore.

The Moulmein (H61) and the Mino received a number of hits but all fortunately above the waterline.

The Mino (H799) like the Crane was built in 1903 at Goole. She and the Moulmein received a number of direct hits.

owners, Messrs. Kelsall Bros. and Beeching. Every man on board was appalled by the unusual nature of the catastrophe, and it was with some difficulty that Captain Peaker told his extraordinary story.

"On Friday midnight', he said, 'there were about forty of the Gamecock fleet of steam trawlers fishing in the North Sea in latitude 55.15 N and longtitude 55.65. That means we were south-east of the Dogger Bank. It was a misty, drizzly night, and we were spread over an area of some miles. Between eleven and twelve o' clock the admiral of the fishing fleet had, according to custom, signalled by rockets and coloured lights what direction the fleet was to sail for during the night. Whether that had anything to do with what followed, I do not know. The whole thing is a mystery. But presently we saw, through the mist and the rain, a number of lights of vessels, big and small. Knowing the Baltic fleet was about to sail, and seeing these ships were steering direct towards the Channel, we naturally assumed that they were the Russians. But as a matter of common honesty, I could not tell you at this moment what ships

General view of the Gamecock fleet off the Dogger Bank when fired on by the Baltic Squadron (The Graphic).

they were. All I know is that there were many of them, that they were signalling towards one another with lights, and that with their powerful searchlights they spied out every one of our fleet. Suddenly some of the warships started firing at us - or rather, at about twenty boats which were nearest to them. At first we naturally supposed they were firing blank shot, and the boatswain of the *Tomtit*, which was quite close in, picked up two big fish in his hands and held them out at arms-length. Some say he had been offering the fish to the Russian sailormen, others think they knew that we were peaceful fishermen and not enemies masked as trawlers.

Bosun of the Tomtit holding up two codfish to demonstrate that they were a fleet of fishing boats.

For that matter, the warships were so near to some of the boats that with glasses and searchlights they could easily have seen the men on deck gutting the fish, for that is what all the boats were doing when the first shots were fired.

We were staggered when we began to realise that we were being fired at in earnest, and that the shots were well aimed and wounding men and damaging the trawlers. All was confusion and terror. Some of the boats were in the act of hauling up their trawls when the bombardment began, and they cut away the nets, got up steam and hurried away as fast as they could.

I think the firing lasted about half an hour, and that it was from quick-firing guns on board the cruisers, judging by the rapidity of the shots. I have seen some of the shots which were embedded in the boats. They were about the size and length of a big cucumber and had brass heads on them. I think they are not explosive shells, but I am ignorant of such matters.

What with the darkness and the rain we could not see the Russian boats, only their side-lights, and that they were big vessels, and the big searchlights also helped to blind us. We were quite helpless. We could do nothing to explain our real character, and it seemed as if we would all be sunk one after another without a word of explanation. But happily, after about 30 minutes firing during which dozens and dozens of shots were aimed at us, the guns suddenly ceased, and the fleet steamed speedily towards the Channel. Why they left off, whether they had come to the conclusion that they had made a mistake, I do not know. I say the whole thing was a terrible mystery to us then and now. The one of our fleet to suffer most from the attack was the trawler *Crane*. The skipper of the *Crane* had his head completely blown off with a shot, and another killed the mate, slicing half his head off from chin to hair. All of our crew were wounded, some seriously, and the

NORTH SEA INCIDENT

The dead being transferred to the trawler Moulmein (The Graphic).

boatswain had his left hand blown away.

Nobody knew that at the time, though groanings were heard, and presently it was seen that the *Crane* was settling down, so the skipper of the *Gull*, which was nearest to her, at once launched his boat and boarded the *Crane*. He told me the decks presented a shocking sight, with blood all about, the headless trunk of the captain and the ghastly body of the mate, which was faceless, and the wounded men lying about in such shelter as they had managed to crawl to.

Now the captain of the *Gull* only accounted to me for eight men of the *Crane*. That is, the two dead officers and six wounded men. [4] According to the equipment there should have been nine men on board. Whether the other has gone to the bottom of the sea with the boat I don't know. I don't like to think. The low skunks! The cursed murderers!'

The captain suddenly lost control of himself as his mind went back to the horrors of the night, and his face went purple with passion. It was some minutes before he could continue.

'Well anyway', he said, 'both the dead and wounded men were taken off the *Crane* just in time, for she foundered a few minutes later. She had holes in her sides, through which the water rushed in a torrent. The wounded were placed aboard the Mission's ship *Joseph and Sarah Miles*, which doused her lights, though the Russians were far enough away then.

The two dead men were decently covered up on the *Gull* and taken to Hull, which I reckon would be reached about five o'clock this afternoon. Several other trawlers were damaged by shot. The *Mino* had eight gunshots between wind and water, and the crew had to stuff bedding into the holes to keep her afloat. Luckily the shots had glanced upwards instead of downwards, or she would have sunk. And of course I don't know yet whether she has been able to make Hull. When I left for London there were three or four trawlers unaccounted for, and they may have gone to the bottom.

One boat had her mainsail torn with shot, and in another a shot entered the galley, whizzing

Moulmein, flag at half mast, bringing the victims of the attack into St Andrew's Dock, Hull. (The Graphic)

past the head of the cook, who was putting a kettle on the stove, and went through the ship's side. It is useless', said Captain Peaker in conclusion, 'for anyone to think that torpedo destroyers could be got up to look like trawling vessels. The whole build of the fleet is quite distinctive and easily recognisable.

Each boat carried her lights as required by the Board of Trade rules - a Duplex lamp, showing white right ahead, red on the port side and green on the starboard, together with a white all-round globe at the masthead. I think the Russians lost their heads, blazed away in confusion, and then steamed off when they got no reply and knew us to be harmless fishing folk."

The *Mino* did in fact return to port along with the *Moulmein* on the Sunday afternoon. Joseph Alfred Smith the fifteen-year-old son of George Henry Smith the deceased skipper of the *Crane*, was making his first fishing trip and was the only member of the crew to survive the ordeal without injury. He and the skippers of the *Mino* and *Moulmein* left Hull at 7.45pm on the same day, Sunday 23 October, so as to be able to make a statement to government officials on the Monday morning.

A telegram of protest was sent to the prime-minister by the mayor, Alderman Jarman, who used the now familiar expression 'Russian Outrage,' which also appears in the headline of the *Hull Daily Mail*, Monday 24 October:

'Right Hon. A.J. Balfour, Prime Minister, Downing Street, London.
Greatest indignation prevails here at unprecedented attack on Hull fishing fleet by

THE LATE MR. GEORGE SMITH, SKIPPER OF THE TRAWLER CRANE
Who was killed by a shot from the Baltic Fleet, and his wife.
Photo by J. Towler, Hull.

The late George Smith, (skipper of the Crane) and his wife; a photograph by J. Towler of Hull, reproduced in The Graphic.

Dr Hirjee Anklesaria, surgeon aboard the mission ship Joseph and Sarah Miles (The Graphic).

The Mino in the Hull Fish Dock, skipper Walter Whelpton on the right. The shell-holed top of the companionway was given to the Chief Constable of Hull, who later presented it to the museum.

Skipper Whelpton, left, and crew of Mino. This postcard, published by Valentine's, has been doctored to exaggerate the damage to the companion hood.

11

NORTH SEA INCIDENT

Trawler Moulmein; hole in the casing above the galley indicated by white cross.

Trawler Gull which rescued the dead and wounded from the sinking Crane.

The Moulmein and her crew.

Russian warships resulting in loss of valuable lives.

We appeal to the government to take the speediest and strongest means to ensure full redress and complete security against further Russian outrage.

William Jarman
Mayor of Hull'. [5]

Sir H. Seymour King and Dr T.C. Jackson, with George Beeching, trawler owner, were interviewed at the foreign office. Dr Jackson, of the firm of Andrew Marvel Jackson, was solicitor for Kelsall Bros. and Beeching, and Sir Henry Seymour King, a personal friend, was Conservative Member of Parliament for Central Hull as well as being senior member of H.S. King and Co, East India agents and bankers. The delegation included skipper T. Smith of the *Ava*, Walter Whelpton and J.T. Hames, skippers of the *Mino* and *Moulmein* respectively, but none of these key witnesses were invited to a personal meeting with either the minister or his officials.

The s.t. *Gull* arrived in Hull on the Tuesday evening, and three of the injured from the *Crane* were disembarked and taken by horse ambulance for treatment in the Reckitt Ward of the Royal Infirmary, Prospect Street. These men, who had been transferred back from the mission ship, were William Smith, mate, with a large fragment of shell in his back; Arthur Rea, second engineer, wounded in the chest; and Albert Almond, trimmer, with a piece of shell in his forearm. Still on board the mission ship were John Ryder, deck-hand, wounded in the thigh; John Nixon, chief engineer, badly injured in the back of the head; and Henry Hoggart, the boatswain, with his hand shot away above the wrist. [6] An affidavit recording the eyewitness account of the mate of the *Crane* was taken down by A.M. Jackson and Co. solicitors : [7]

"WILLIAM SMITH of 6 Edwards Terrace, Massey Street, Hull.

I am a fisherman. I am 31 years of age and hold a Certificate of Competency as mate.

On Friday night the 21st October 1904, I was Mate of the steam trawler *Crane,* belonging to Messrs. Kelsall Bros & Beeching Ltd of Hull. We had been with the Fleet a month and 5 days and during that time we had not seen or heard of any strangers or Japanese, or any warships or strange craft being with the Fleet.

We were to windward of the Admiral's ship, about midnight on the 21st Octobe, and the *Gull* was astern of us, a little on our lee quarter. I do not know which way we were heading because I had only just come on deck and had not been on the bridge. It had been my watch below up to hauling time.

I saw the first division of warships pass us astern, some distance off, and the first intimation we had that they were warships was by seeing searchlights from them. The first I saw was that 3 searchlights were turned on us from a ship that was on our port bow. This ship fired on us and hit us. He then sheered across our head and fired at our starboard side. The ship following fired at our port side, so that we were between a crossfire. I do not know where our ship was first hit.

When the Russians opened fire, we had our regulation fishing lights up - that is, the triplex light at the masthead, with a white light underneath it and a stern light. There were also two deck lights in the fish pound to enable us to see to gut fish. We had our mizzen set. There were four of us in the fish pound, but three of the men went out of the fish pound when the firing started and went forward. I continued gutting the fish for a few minutes and then went out of the pound and found a piece of shell close besides me on the deck. I picked this up, but it was too hot to hold in my hand.

I then went aft to put my knife in the lamp locker, and when passing the winch I saw the chief engineer (Nixon) under the lee of the bridge. He said 'Bill, I am hit'. I took my sponge cloth off my neck and gave it to him and told him to put it round his neck. I saw blood streaming from his head. The Skipper then came down from the bridge and I said to him 'Poor old Jack has got hit'. He said 'For God's sake what are they doing? I said I did not know.

Someone then called out from forward that the Boatswain was hit.

I then went forward, and as I was passing the winch something hit me on my back and stunned me for a second or two, knocking me down. I crawled forward and went to the forecastle companion and found the Boatswain, Hoggart, with his right hand shattered. I left him there and went aft to see the Skipper and when I got abreast of the winch I found him laid on the fore side of the bridge near the grating. I took hold of him and found he was dead, with his head all shattered. I then went aft and saw the Chief Engineer standing against the cabin companion and told him the Skipper was dead. Someone then told me the ship was making water fast. I then went forward to get the boat out and found Leggett laid against the forecastle door, dead.

I found all the crew were crippled and that I could not get any help. I jumped into the boat and put the plug in and carried the painter end to the winch. I tried to heave her out, but found I could not get any steam. I examined the winch and found it all shattered. The firing was still going on and lasted, I should think, fully 20 minutes.

When I found I could not get the boat out I went to the bridge, intending to steer the vessel towards the nearest trawler. The firing was just ceasing. I found the steering gear had been shattered. The 2nd Engineer then came on deck to stop the steam escaping from the whistle pipe (which had been shattered) and I told him to stop the engines and he went back into the engine room, which was in total darkness.

I therefore got on the deck again and took a white deck light and waved it from the side towards the *Gull* to draw his attention that I was in distress. All our other lights had been shot out. I then went to the lamp locker and found a red lamp, which was the only one left in the locker which had not been shattered. I lit it with a struggle and waved it up and down for assistance. The trawler came round close up to us and hailed us. I recognised the Skipper's voice and shouted 'Green, get your boat out, for God's sake, we are all broke up'.

All the lights on deck and below had been shot out. The boat from the *Gull* came alongside and Costello, the boatswain, came on board. I then told Smith to get in first, then the decky, then the trimmer, the boatswain, 2nd and chief engineer. The Boatswain of the *Gull* assisted me in putting all the wounded in the boat. I was feeling very bad, as I was losing a lot of blood and so I asked the Chief Engineer of the *Gull* (who was in the boat) to come to assist Costello and myself in getting the Skipper and 3rd Hand into the boat. We all three assisted in getting the Skipper into the boat and Costello, followed by Smirk and myself, went forward and down into the forecastle and lifted the body of Leggett up so that I could get hold of his hands and drag him on deck. We then placed him in the boat. Costello and Smirk then got into the boat and I left the ship, being the last. The *Crane* was then fast settling down by her stern.

We were taken on board the *Gull* and in about 5 minutes time I saw the *Crane* sink.

The engineer of the *Gull* attended to our wounds as well as he could, and we were later transferred to the mission ship *Joseph and Sarah Miles* and attended by the doctor. On the Sunday we were put on board the mission ship *Alpha* and later on re-transferred to the *Gull*, which brought us to Hull."

The *Joseph and Sarah Miles* had a sick berth in the charge of Dr. Hirjee N. Anklesaria equipped with six beds, including two swinging cots, surgical apparatus and an X-ray machine. In addition to the surgeon was a complement of twelve men - the captain, two engineers and nine hands - so that the vessel could actively engage in fishing as well as providing medical assistance for the trawlermen at work in the North Sea. The mission ship remained on station with the fleet until Tuesday 28 October, by which time the two men killed aboard the *Crane* had been buried. She arrived at Hull at 3.30 in the morning.   John Ryder, John Dixon and Harry Hoggart disembarked and the latter was sent to London for further treatment. [8] No-one it seems had bothered to inform his wife of this decision and she was left waiting at the infirmary in a state of some distress, without seeing for herself what condition he was in. Though in very good hands, since the King himself had asked the eminent surgeon Sir Frederick Treves to be present whilst he was undergoing treatment, Hoggart's wife was still, on the 30 October, in the dark concerning his state of health.

In fact, the bosun's forearm had been removed whilst at sea, and later a surgeon of the London hospital located and removed a shell splinter. [9]

On Thursday 27 October there was a mass of people lining the streets, along the Park Street Bridge and all the way to the cemetery on Spring Bank. Fishermen dressed in the regalia of the Royal Antediluvian Order of Buffaloes (a friendly society popular in the fishing community) over their blue jerseys gathered outside the home of the late Skipper Smith in Ribble Avenue. The coffin was brought out through the window and placed on trestles, whereupon Capt. White, leader of the Fishermen's Association, gave out the first two lines of 'Lead Kindly Light'. [10] The bandsmen of the Buffaloes, assembled at the corner of Ribble and Tyne Streets since 2pm, immediately began to play and the coffin put onto a horse-

Funeral cortege of Skipper Smith and William Leggett, 27 October, 1904.

drawn hearse for the solemn procession to the burial ground. In the lead was the Chief Constable of Hull, Major Malcolm, [11] mounted on a horse, followed by the Buffaloes band members of the Salvation Army with their band. Then came the hearse of Skipper Smith, the mourners, followed by thirty members of the

Removing the coffin of Skipper Smith from his house at 7 Ribble Avenue, Ribble Street, Hull; from The People, Sunday 30 October, 1904.

Hark to the mourners' weeping,
Sobb'd with 'bated breath.
Whilst in anguish keeping,
Watch o'er those whose death
Came while perils scorning
On the mighty deep—
Night—o'er shadow'd morning,
Marshalling death's long sleep.

List to the indignation,
From men of every tongue;
The mighty British nation,
Whose heart's deep chords are wrung.
Hark to the children's crying,
List to the widow's prayers.
Daughter of Fair Britannia,
A Nation's grief is theirs.

God His watch is keeping,
O'er the children's tears,
Daughters of Fair Britannia,
Calm with love their fears.
Help the lonely widow
To lock within the breast,
Her sorrow and her anguish,
Remembering—God knows best.
—REGINALD T. SHUTTE.

Interred at Western Cemetery, Spring Bank, Hull, October 27th, at 3·15 p.m.

To the Memory of

THE HULL FISHERMEN,
GEORGE H. SMITH & JOHN LEGGOTT,
who lost their Lives through the
Russian Baltic Fleet Blunder,
on the Dogger Bank, on
— OCTOBER 21st., 1904. —

Cards to commemorate Skipper Smith and William Leggett which were on sale at the time of the funeral; the latter's name is sometimes wrongly recorded as John instead of William.

Sacred

TO THE MEMORY OF

THE HONOURED DEAD
Captain Smith,
and Third hand Leggott,
Who were Shot & and their vessel the
Steam trawler the Crane wantonally
Shelled and Sunk by Russian War
Ships, in the North Sea.
October 22nd, 1904.

Contented the Fishermen smiled,
For the Angel of Peace seemed about
When Demons let loose without warning
The lives of two men blotted out!

The two identical memorials of Skipper Smith (left) and William Leggett (right) and the black marble headstone (behind) of Walter Whelpton, who died in 1905. Contemporary postcard photograph, Western Cemetery, Hull.

In
Loving Memory of
My dear Husband
Capt George Henry
Smith,
Who was killed on the ill faird
Trawler Crane, by the
Russian Baltic Fleet, in the
North Sea, Octr 22nd 1904,
Aged 40 Years.

We cannot Lord, thy purpose see
But all is well that's done by Thee

In
Loving Memory of
My dear Son
William Richard
Leggett,
Who was killed on the ill faird
Trawler Crane, by the
Russian Baltic Fleet, in the
North Sea Octr 22nd 1904,
Aged 28 Years.

In the midst of life we are
in Death.

In Loving Memory of
My dear Husband
Capt Walter Whelpton,
Of the Trawler Jane
Who died Mch 15th 1905,
Through short illness caused by the
Russian Baltic Fleet in the North Sea
Octr 22nd 1904,
Aged 50 Years.
Peace, perfect Peace

Details of the inscriptions on the headstones.

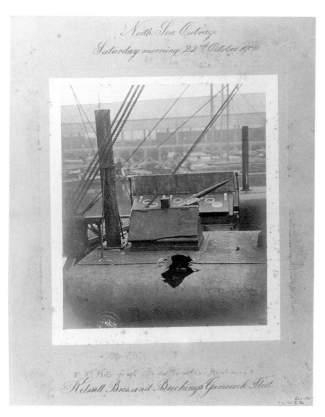

The s.t. Moulmein. One of a series of official photographs of the damaged trawlers taken by Turner and Drinkwater, Hull, bearing the stamp of the Medical Offices Dept, Town Hall, Hull.

crew of HMS *Hearty,* RNR, men of the Gamecock fleet, the owners and directors, and after them the coffin of William Leggett, his mourners and, lastly, the mayor and corporation, and men of the police force mounted and on foot.

George Henry Smith was forty years old and Leggett only twenty-eight. A Norfolk man from Gorleston, he had sailed out of Yarmouth until March 1903. Mourned by his parents, the young man's remains had been taken from the house of an acquaintance living in Floral Avenue, Westbourne Street, along to Tyne Street to await the cortege. Mr L. Spring and Mr J.H. Robins of the Hull Fishing Vessel Owners' Association were there with representatives of the Humber Amalgamated Steam Trawler Engineers' and Firemen's Union, and the Hull Seamen's and Marine Firemen's Amalgamated Society. The bearers of Smith's coffin were fishermen of the Blythe Boys branch of the R.A.O.B., of which he had been a member, and the column moved slowly and deliberately on its way to the notes of the dead march played alternately by the two bands. Except for the too-raucous cries of a street vendor selling memorial cards, 'only a penny', no-one seems to have offended against the solemnity of the occasion.

The Russian Fleet and the Russo-Japanese War

To understand the events of the 21-22 October it is necessary to gain some idea of the reasons for the Russian-Japanese war and of the level of competence and morale of the crews aboard the vessels of the Russian fleet. The whole dreadful saga seems at first sight to be unlikely to the point of absurdity and farce, but an examination of the happenings in Russia and on board the vessels of the Baltic fleet reveal an inexorable chain of cause and effect based on misinformation and hysteria. [12]

Over many centuries Russia had spread its influence within the land mass of Asia, its territory spreading from the Baltic to the Pacific. In the age of contending nations wishing to extend their imperium, sea-power, based on trade and the great war-fleets to protect these mercantile interests, was the essence of political power. The supremacy of the Royal Navy had been established at Trafalgar (1805) and Navarino (1827), the last two great fleet engagements in which the British were involved before Jutland in 1917. The mere threat of the existence of great capital ships with their enormous fire-power was enough to retain this British dominance. Most of the naval activity , maintaining colonial control and influence was conducted with numbers of lesser vessels, gunboats, armed river boats and patrolling cruisers.

Other nations sought to establish spheres of influence and Russia, like Germany, was determined to build a presence on the high seas which would be a visible expression of its power. Unfortunately, access to the open sea was greatly restricted. The north coast faced the ice-bound wastes of the Arctic and the North Sea was only reachable through the narrows of the Baltic. Any attempt to dominate Asia Minor and have ready access to the eastern Mediterranean was blocked by the Ottoman Turks, while a warm-water base in the Indian Ocean was prevented by Britain's dominance of the Indian subcontinent. Attempts by Russia to undermine the Raj through the 'Great Game', fomenting trouble in Afghanistan and on the North-West Frontier, proved fruitless. Therefore, the only logical outlet was in the Pacific and the town of Vladivostok, established on the coast of Siberia in 1860, was developed as the Russian naval base in the east, though it still had the disadvantage of being iced up in the winter months. To connect it with the imperial capital and the interior, the Trans-Siberian

railway was begun in 1891. The Chinese Empire, then in its decadence, was too feeble to keep out thrusting new imperial powers which used its weakness to extend their own influence and territory. The Chinese accommodated a short cut for the railway through Manchuria in return for an alliance against Japan.

Kaiser Wilhelm II joined the vultures picking at the remains of a once-proud and ancient civilisation and persuaded the Chinese to allow him to occupy the Shantung peninsular, establishing an ice-free naval base with all-year-round access, at Tsingtao in Chiao-Chou bay.

The Japanese had captured the Liaiotung peninsular in the Sino-Japanese war of 1894-5 and were then forced to relinquish it by the Western powers. Russia, in turn, acquired a lease in 1898 and the right to build a railway linking with the Chinese railway at Harbin through to the Trans-Siberian Railroad. A heavily fortified naval base was constructed at Port Arthur (Lu-shun), which unlike Vladivostok was never ice-bound. The Russian presence temporarily thwarted Japanese ambitions to establish control of Korea and led to the Russo-Japanese war. Japan declared war on the 8th February 1904 and Port Arthur was besieged on land and blockaded from the sea. The Russian battleship *Petropavlosk* was sunk by a mine in March (with the death of Admiral Makarov and Grand Duke Kyril) and accummulating losses resulted in a demand for replacements to strengthen the Russian naval forces operating out of Port Arthur and Vladivostok.

In response to this threatening situation the

Baltic fleet was assembled at St Petersburg to be sent to the Far East as the Second Pacific Squadron, headed by four battleships- *Kniaz Suvorov* (the flagship), *Borodino, Alexander III* and *Orel*- all newly completed vessels of the Borodino class, twin-funnelled with 12 inch guns and capable of a speed of 18 knots. [13] The contingent of forty-two vessels, made up of warships and auxiliaries, including supply and repair vessels, was to sail 18,000 miles under the command of Admiral Zinovi Petrovich Rozhestvensky. Then aged fifty-five (born 30 October 1848, the son of a military doctor) he was an experienced veteran with a special aptitude for naval gunnery. He had been

Admiral Rozhestvensky, commander of the Russian Baltic fleet.

Russian naval attaché in London in 1892 and had been second in command of the *Vesta*, a small-armed steamer of the Black Sea fleet in action against the Turks. He commanded Admiral Alexiev's flagship in the Far East at the time of the Sino-Japanese war and was then transferred to St Petersburg, where he was placed in charge of the gunnery practice squadron of the Baltic fleet. In 1902 Rozhestvensky was appointed chief of naval staff and aide-de-camp to the Tsar.

Despite the efforts of Tsar Peter the Great (1672-1725), imperial Russia never established a sound naval tradition. A small core of well-trained officers was more than counterbalanced by placemen and political appointees and a mass of recruits whose training was inadequate to transform them from peasant farmers into effective sailors. The icing up of the Baltic ports restricted sea drill to only half the year and the raising of such a task force in just a few months meant that it was overwhelmed with hastily recalled reservists and merchant seamen unused to naval discipline. Most of the best men with battle experience were already serving in the Pacific and a large number of these were caught up in the blockade of Port Arthur by the Japanese fleet. To add to all this there was considerable civil unrest and a display of revolutionary fervour, which spilled over into the services with the result that there were many, including some officers, quite willing to see the expedition end in a debacle. Seldom can there have been a less satisfactory start to a major naval enterprise.

In addition to the problems of personnel, there were also serious doubts about the actual ships.

The Borodino class ships were notoriously top-heavy and when heavily loaded the lower decks were almost awash. They were accompanied by three older, slower and less heavily armed battleships, *Osliabia*, *Sissoi Veliky* and *Navarin*. An armoured cruiser, the *Dmitri Donskoi*, dating from 1883, had originally been rigged for sail and the *Svetlana* resembled a hybrid between a cruiser and a steam yacht. There were, however, four modern fast cruisers, *Oleg*, *Aurora*, *Jemtchug* and *Izumrud* and a number of torpedo-boat destroyers. [14]

Attempts in early September to bring some order and discipline into the fleet were not encouraging. Whilst off Reval (Tallinn), at two o'clock one morning the Admiral ordered the officer of the watch to issue the signal for defence against torpedo boat attack. Eight minutes later there was no response, all the officers and men were asleep and when a few hands of the watch finally appeared they had no idea what to do.

Torpedoes were the most feared naval weapon of the period and had been developed to a considerable level of effectiveness since the first successful design was offered for sale in 1866 by Robert Whitehead, a British engineer. This self-propelled underwater explosive device was utilised by launching it from small, fast boats, which were highly manoeuvrable and presented difficult targets for larger, slower cruisers and battleships. As a result, the torpedo-boat destroyer was developed as a countermeasure, equipped with guns and torpedoes and with a speed equal to or greater than its adversaries. The torpedo, however, achieved its deadliest results in two World Wars when launched from a submarine and delivered to its target entirely underwater, unseen and unheralded.

Route of the Second Pacific Squadron, October 11-23, 1904

The assembled fleet left Kronstadt bound for Reval (Tallin) and the official send-off but one of the battleships, the *Orel*, drawing nearly twenty-nine feet, ran aground in the shallows and it took a days dredging to cut a passage for her through the mud. After two day's of intensive polishing, scrubbing and cleaning the fleet was reviewed by Tsar Nicholas II and set sail thirty-six hours later on the 13 October. A last call was made at Libau (Lepaya) for coal on the 15th and then the armada set forth on what would prove an epic and tragic voyage. There immediately followed a catalogue of incidents; the *Sissoi Veliky* lost her anchor, a destroyer rammed the *Osliabia* and the *Orel* had trouble with her engines and steering. In an attempt to jolt a little sense into his commanders, the Admiral had frequent recourse to firing blank charges at the offending vessels and on one occasion, when a signal was ignored ,a live shell was put across a ship's bows!

All sorts of rumours were circulating in the fleet about Japanese spies and saboteurs active on the Danish and Norwegian coasts, of torpedo boats disguised as trawlers lurking in the fjords and mines laid in the narrows. There was no actual evidence to support these stories, but much of the misinformation probably emanated from German sources, part of the ongoing diplomatic and political assault on Russia. An uncritical Russian intelligence service, eager to demonstrate its efficiency, transmitted this farrago, probably aided by dissident Russians trying to spread fear and alarm.

The feelings of vulnerability were no doubt exacerbated by knowledge of the alliance between Britain and Japan, signed in London on the 30 January 1902, to assist one another in safeguarding their respective interests in China and Korea. There had been cooperation over a number of years - many officers of the Japanese navy had trained in England, including Admiral Togo the present commander-in-chief. In 1901 the capital ship *Hatsuse* was built at Armstrong's yard on the Tyne at Elswick, preceded by the cruiser *Idzume* in 1900 and the latter's sister ship *Iwate* in 1901. At the time of the North Sea Outrage the battleship *Koshima* was also under construction at Elswick. In addition, the Entente Cordiale between Britain and France, agreed on the 8 April 1904, threatened the alliance between Russia and France. To add to all these worries, internal unrest resulted in the murder of Viacheslav Plehve, the Russian Minister of the Interior, 28 July 1904, when preparations of the Baltic fleet were in full swing.

Intelligence reports were passed to Rozhestvensky which stated that the Russian fleet was likely to be ambushed on its way through the Baltic. It was claimed Japanese officers had been despatched to the Baltic Sea coast and armed with torpedoes. An agent to the Russian naval attaché in France had apparently got hold of samples of coal briquettes, hollowed out for explosives, which if put in a ship's furnace would do immense damage.

Unidentified torpedo boats were reported off Skagen, where the fleet was to anchor for coaling. The Danes were friendly to Russia - King Charles IX was grandfather of Nicholas II and the latter's mother, the Empress Dowager Maria Fiodorovna, was at the time taking a holiday in Denmark. Formerly the Danish princess Dagmar, fourth child of Christian IX, she was sister to Queen Alexandra, wife of King Edward VII.

A Danish squadron was sent to guard the straits between the Baltic and the North Sea ,while on shore two Japanese, suspected of being agents, were detained when they tried to hire a boat. There were further reports of Japanese boats in the North Sea having left hiding places in the Norwegian fjords.

It is interesting to note that the *Illustrated London News* (3 December 1904 p.812) records the despatch of a torpedo boat from England to Russia, bought and smuggled by a Mr Sinnett, an Irish sympathiser. Knowing the Russian fleet was in great need of such vessels, he took it upon himself to overcome the deficiency. Presenting himself as the agent of an American millionaire who required a very fast yacht, he persuaded the builders (Palmer's) to sell him a torpedo boat for £25,000. Named *Caroline*, the craft was then completely disguised to match her supposed role as a pleasure boat and on the 6 October started her 30-knot dash across the North Sea. Arriving at Cuxhaven on the 8th October she then passed through the Kiel Canal, with the pilot becoming extremely suspicious. He went ashore to report her to the authorities, but the *Caroline* made a rapid departure, ignoring the signals to stop, and was soon handed over to the Russian Navy.

Whether this report is authentic or just another example of rumour and the overheated and exaggerated 'intelligence' circulating at the time the present author has not confirmed. In reality it seems not a single spy or agent had been sent to this area by the Japanese and certainly no armed vessels of any kind, but such was the tension and alarm generated by these reports that watches were doubled and men stood by their guns. Any approaching merchantman or fishing vessel was promptly signalled off, and on more than one occasion hastened on their way by the occasional shot. On the 18th October there was an attempt to sweep for mines the narrow channel leading to the entrance of the Great Belt. This crude and ineffectual undertaking was abandoned, but needless to say none of the ships encountered any mines.

It must have been some consolation to Rozhestvensky, amidst the worry and strain of leading such a lubberly command, to receive a telegram from the Tsar announcing his advancement to the rank of vice-admiral. The suggestive state of the Russian crews was further emphasised when, before sailing past Skagen, the lookouts of the *Navarin* claimed to have sighted two balloons. These were supposed to be making a reconnaissance, giving the squadron's position to a waiting enemy flotilla! On the 21st October the *Kamchatka*, which had become separated from the fleet by engine trouble, reported being chased by torpedo boats and that she was firing on them. The *Suvorov* was suspicious of further messages received over the radio, imagining some trickery by the Japanese and when two flares were suddenly reported from the bridge, searchlights were swung in their direction and the 'engage enemy' signal given. A hail of fire ensued and a group of small vessels, with a larger one amongst them, was caught in the beam of the searchlights. The *Orel* ran out of loaded and primed twelve-pounder shells, then suddenly more lights switched on sweeping over the battleships and muzzle-flashes were observed. At first these were thought to be Japanese reinforcements coming on the scene, but the pattern of radio signals was identified as friendly and it became apparent aboard the *Suvorov* that they were receiving fire from cruisers of Admiral Enkvist's division. The buglers aboard the flagship ordered the general ceasefire and the searchlights were switched off, except for one beam pointing upwards as the signal to break off action.

The time was five minutes to one and the warships steamed away at full speed to the south after an engagement lasting some fifteen minutes. All lights were extinguished in fear of further attacks, but there was a general feeling of intense excitement that the 'enemy' had been beaten off. Morale was high and the gunners felt a confidence that had not been present before. Left behind them in the North Sea was a tragic scene of death and confusion as the Hull fishing fleet tried to comprehend what had occasioned this unprovoked attack.

The affidavit of John Allan, skipper of the *Oceanic* tells the following story : [15]

"John Allan of 5 Pretoria Avenue, Edinburgh Street, Hessle Road, Hull.

I am 32 years of age and I have been about eighteen years engaged in fishing, seven years with steam trawlers. I have been a skipper nine years. I was born in Dundee. I am Skipper of the steam trawler *Oceanic*, owned by Messrs. Kelsall Bros and Beeching Ltd of Hull. Our number is H449, painted in large white letters on both bows, and name on stern; a white flag with red cock is painted on both sides of funnel.

We left Hull on the 4th October to join the Gamecock fleet in the North Sea. On Friday evening the 21st October inst. we were fishing with the fleet about 200 miles E by W of Spurn. The wind was South-South-East, the weather fine, a bit hazy up above.

We had hauled our trawl and about a quarter to 12 by our clock, which was an hour and half fast, we shot it again at about quarter past twelve by our clock in about 23 fathoms of water, towing on the starboard tack. Heading ENE, wind and weather same as before. At this time the Admiral's ship *Ruff* was on our port bow about 200 yards off. She was also on the starboard tack. I could see his lights. Our ship is about 102 feet long.

There was another trawler on the starboard beam. I did not know the name at the time, but afterwards when she hailed us during the firing I found that she was the *Moulmein*. I could see her lights all the time. There were a good many trawlers around and in the vicinity of the Admiral's vessel, as usually happens. There were also a good many trawlers astern of us, also a certain number, but not so very many, on our starboard. There were a lot of them also on the port side, some way off.

We were showing the usual trawling lights, viz red, white and green and globular white lights on the foremast and a white stern light. We had at this time finished gutting the fish and had no deck lights. About half an hour after shooting our gear, I saw a searchlight on our port bow and then noticed the steaming lights of three or four large vessels on our port bow about a mile and a half off. I at first thought that they were large cargo vessels. They kept coming on till they got on our port quarter and commenced signalling one to the other, beginning with the lead vessel and I then came to the conclusion that they were warships. The first lot of signals appeared to be 4 white lights, suddenly lit up and then went out - this happened three times all at the same place on the ship - then two white lights appeared in the same place and then I saw four mixed lights - red, white and green - in same place and ended with a red and white light; the vessels following the leader appeared to repeat these signals or something like them. A few searchlights were shown by these warships and the ships apparently stopped on our port quarter. I then noticed four or five more warships coming across our fleet head and crossing to our starboard bow - they had the usual steaming lights. Three of four of them, including the leading vessel, turned their search lights on us;they were moving slowly, and when the leading vessel got on our starboard quarter she commenced firing and the second ship did the same. All the vessels seemed to stop.

I saw a green rocket go up from the Admiral's vessel just before the firing began and I saw three or four more sent up by him during the firing. A green rocket means 'continue to trawl on the starboard tack' and I kept on that tack. The mizzen sail was set, but the mainsail stowed. The shots from the vessel were falling in the water all around us and passing over our heads- close by I could hear their whistle; we were fishing 200 yards to a quarter of a mile away from the headmost vessel.

About three-quarters of the way through the firing the *Moulmein*, who had been heading the same way as we had on our starboard quarter, turned on her port side and headed across our stern. Someone on board shouted out that she was shot; I shouted back to him to keep his vessel to or he would come into my gear and I put on full speed to try to clear her, but she must must have caught our trawl as it was gone when we hauled up at 7.30 next morning.

The *Moulme*in went off to leeward of us and we did not see her again till next morning. Shortly after *Moulmein* passed to the leeward of us, the warships stopped firing,; we were about abreast of the third warship when they stopped firing.

After they stopped firing, the warships went off to the SW and I saw no more of any of them. I went down to my supper as soon as I saw them go off.

One vessel has gone on the slip to be looked at. I could not see the colour of the warships nor any flag on them - we were blinded by the searchlights. They seemed to be firing mostly from the decks.

There were no torpedo boats, Japanese or otherwise, in our fleet at any time, nor any Japanese men on board - we should all have known it if there were any. We had not been approached by anyone to do any harm to the Russian fleet.

We carried no guns or small arms not even for signalling. Trawlers don't. The sound of the Admiral's signal rocket is not a bit like the report of a gun. The rockets came down in three balls. I heard no bugle on board the warship.

John Allan".

The attack had started with the shots fired by the *Kamchatka* on the trawler *Tomtit* which was separated from the main group of fishing vessels. A cluster of boats with the mission ship *Alpha*, the larger vessel amongst the trawlers, observed by the *Suvarov*, came under attack as an immediate response to the green rockets sent up by the 'admiral' of the fishing fleet. These were just part of the normal repertory of signals used on the fishing grounds to direct the movements of the trawlers under the 'admiral's' command. [16]

The *Orel* had loosed off more than five hundred twelve-pounder shells and during the action the supply of primed and loaded shells had been used up. Both the *Aurora* and *Dmitri Donskoi* had received hits in the upper works from rounds fired by other Russian vessels.

Aboard the former a gunner had been injured and Chaplain Afanasy mortally wounded by a 45mm shell. The various reports from the trawler crews indicate that the hits came not from the main turret guns, but from quick-firing guns and machine guns.

The trawling fleet was a combined one comprising about thirty Gamecock vessels belonging to Kelsall Bros. and Beeching, along with three carrier boats, twelve of James Leyman's fleet and two mission ships. The *Crane* had been sunk, the *Mino* and *Moulmein* seriously damaged and the *Gull, Snipe* and *Majestic* and the *Alpha* were affected to a lesser extent. Later there were reports of other vessels being fired on - the foreign trawler *Sonntag* at 8.30pm on the evening of the 21 October and ss *Aldebaran* of Helsingborg, a Swedish steamer, the same evening.

These were doubtless victims of the *Kamchatka*, the floating workshop, the eccentric behaviour of which became notorious throughout the Russian fleet. Her actions were crucial in initiating the bombardment of the Hull fishing vessels.

There was an immense public outcry and in London the Russian embassy was the scene of noisy protests. In the meantime the Second Pacific Squadron steamed through the English Channel and the Admiral began to realise that his actions had created an international incident with the serious threat of war. Rozhestvensky sent a telegram giving his version of the events:

"The incident of the North Sea was provoked by two torpedo-boats which, without showing any lights, under cover of darkness advanced to attack the vessel steaming at the head of the detachment. When the detachment began to sweep the sea with its searchlights, and opened fire, the presence was also discovered of several small fishing vessels. The detachment endeavoured to spare these boats" [17]

This unrepentant communication was followed by a second telegram which suggested it was unwise of foreign fishing vessels to involve themselves in this enterprise by enemy torpedo boats but 'in the name of the whole fleet, to express our sincere regret for the unfortunate victims of circumstances in which no warship could, even in times of profound peace, have acted otherwise.' [18] *The Times* on the 25th

October, demanded justice backed by all the power of the empire, and Sir Charles Hardinge, British Ambassador in St Petersburg, handed in a strong note of protest demanding an apology and an assurance that the guilty officers would be punished. Later in the day Count Lamsdorff, Russian minister for foreign affairs, called at the Embassy with a request to pass on to King Edward and the government the Tsar's sincere regret. The Russian Admiralty remained obdurate and the fleet continued on its way south.

War fever mounted with the announcement that the Mediterranean, Channel and Home fleets were to be put in a state of readiness, and by the 26th October there were no less than twenty-eight battleships with steam up or already at sea, prepared to intercept and destroy the Second Pacific Squadron at a word from Whitehall.

On the 28 October the prime minister, Arthur Balfour, made a speech at Southampton in which he stated the Russian fleet would be detained at Vigo pending the outcome of an inquiry. This was to be conducted by an international court, and in order to achieve an acceptable settlement it was necessary to receive expressions of profound regret for this flagrant assault on unarmed vessels, punishment of the guilty parties and liberal compensation for those who had suffered. The government were thus seen to be taking a firm stand and, now there was time for reflection, overheated emotions began to cool and the threat of war subsided quite quickly. Although the Russian ships were supposed to be detained at Vigo, they were allowed to take on coal and sail to Tangiers,

Lord Charles Beresford, Warden of the Channel. The Russian fleet passed through the channel on 29 October.

though they were followed all the way by units of the British fleet which made a great show and harassed them by a variety of close manoeuvres.

Whilst the nation at large was already beginning to forget 'the North Sea Incident,' in Hull the bitterness remained and there was some public criticism of the reactions to the recent events of Charles Henry Wilson, who had been sympathetic to the Russian position from the start, stressing that he was convinced it was a sad blunder rather than a deliberate attack:

'To the editor of the Hull Times

Sir, I should like to express my surprise and disgust at the attitude of Mr C.H. Wilson, the member for West Hull, on the question of the Russian Outrage. Although the poor fellows were his constituents, he not only tries to defend the Russians' cowardly attack but leaves it to our worthy member for Central Hull, Sir H.A. King, to look after the deceased men's families, and to place their case in the hands of the government .. etc.

I am, sir, an East Hull Tradesman.

Hull October 28th 1904.' [19]

Wilson would have been well aware of the state of unrest in St Petersburg and the Baltic States as many of the ships of the Wilson Line traded to the Baltic and the imperial capital. Therefore, he would have been able to understand better than most how the affair might have originated. Equally, he had to protect his trading position and the safety of his vessels and crews when visiting Russian ports. Any speech or public statement made by him in Hull would undoubtedly have eventually been reported in full to Tsarist officials in St Petersburg. At the same time, he had a major investment in the Red Cross fishing fleet, which fortunately had not been involved in the recent events.

Wilson used the opportunity of a stone-laying ceremony at the Congregational Church, Newland, to make a reply to his critics. He made it quite clear that, despite being chairman of the Hull Fishermen's Widows and Orphans fund, member for West Hull, and also chairman of the Hull Seamen's and General Orphanage (for which his father had been chairman forty years before him), he had not been asked to represent the fishermen and their dependants. Sir Seymour King had been in London at the time and he was a personal friend of Dr Jackson, solicitor for the Gamecock fleet.

The coroner's inquest convened in the St George's Hall on the 2 November and its business was completed in a day, with the following verdict : [20]

"That George Henry Smith and William Leggett were, at about 12.30am on October 22, 1904, whilst fishing with trawls out in the North Sea on the Dogger Bank [21] on board the British steam trawler *Crane*, in company with between forty and fifty vessels of the Hull fishing fleet, with the Board of Trade marks exhibited and regulation lights burning, killed by shots fired without warning or provocation, from certain Russian war vessels at a distance of about a quarter of a mile from the said steam trawler *Crane*.

And we further say that the bodies of the said deceased were landed at the St Andrew's Dock in the Parish of Sculcoates in the City and County of Kingston upon Hull on October 23rd last".

In anticipation of compensation, no public relief fund had been set up but a variety of donations had reached the city, starting with £100 from Queen Alexandra and 200 guineas from the King, reported on the 25 October. Lord Ripon gave £100, as did Lord Rothschild, Lord Londesborough £25, and by the 5th November a total of nearly £1000 had been accumulated.

NORTH SEA INCIDENT

Benefit performances at the Grand Theatre, Islington; the Garrick Theatre, Charing Cross Road, the Queen's Theatre, Fleetwood; and by Maskelyne and Cooke's Company at the Egyptian Hall, Piccadilly, all helped to swell the fund.

Spy scares not only helped create the overheated atmosphere in which the tragedy of the North Sea Incident unfolded but persisted afterwards too. John William Tait (clerk to Andrew Jackson, Solicitors) was asked to go out and to inspect the condition of the fleet on the North Sea and interview the survivors of the *Crane* and skipper of the *Moulmein* to gather evidence for the subsequent Board of Trade inquiry. He states that "a few weeks after the preliminary enquiry there were two Russian spies caught amongst our fishermen, and we had to try and find what their object was. One morning these two men got in touch with a skipper who was in the fleet at the time and a deckhand. The Skipper (who was a pretty cute chap) put these two fellows off and made an appointment to meet them later. In the meantime they went and saw Mr George Beeching (one of the owners of the fleet) and he instructed me to find out what these fellows were after.

I, as a matter of fact, got into a fisherman's rig and was introduced to the two men as Bill Johnson - boatswain of the *Rangoon*. I soon found out that their object was to try and get men in the fleet to say that there were strange vessels or some Japanese boats in the fleet - which was all nonsense, of course.

We were asked to meet these two chaps, two big fine looking fellows, next night as soon as dark to go to the Russian Embassy in London. As a matter of fact, we weren't taken to London but to the private house of the then Russian consul in Hull, a man [J. Heard] I knew as well as could be. When we got to his private house we found, in addition to the consul, a gentleman down from the Russian Embassy in London. We had concocted a sort of tale to tell this gentleman.

This didn't leave much doubt what they were up to, so I spread a report on the dock that unless these spies cleared out they'd be thrown in the dock. As a matter of fact, they cleared out under police protection.

Incidentally, two men had given information that there were strange vessels in the fleet. A Russian officer came down to Hull later and, in fact, did leave some money at a hotel there for the two men in question, to take them to the Paris enquiry. But they never turned up for the money to go" (*The Listener*, 1937, p. 537).

2 The Board of Trade Inquiry

On the 15 November the Board of Trade inquiry commenced at the lecture hall of the Hull Assembly Rooms, headed by Admiral Sir Cyprian Bridge and Mr Butler Aspinall KC. A series of eyewitness descriptions were given by the fishermen involved, and four days later the court was adjourned *sine die* to await action by the Board of Trade. The affidavits of William Smith and John Allan transcribed above were probably taken down at this time or they may have been penned soon after returning to Hull from the fishing grounds, when the government was anxiously seeking details of what had occurred.

The essence of the report presented by the commissioners of the Board of Trade is reproduced from the official publication released in 1905 : [22]

Inquiry into the circumstances connected with the North Sea Incident, 21-22 October, 1904

Report from the Commissioners appointed by the Board of Trade

To the RIGHT HONOURABLE GERALD BALFOUR, M.P.,& C.,

Sir,

We have the honour to report that we first visited Hull on 5th November, and inspected the damaged trawlers which were there, and saw the injuries which had been inflicted on them by the gun-fire of warships in the North Sea on the night between the 21st and 22nd October, 1904. The particulars of damage are described in detail in the Appendix.

As soon as the presence of the witnesses could be secured, many having to come in from the fishing ground in the North Sea, we opened an Inquiry in the Lecture Hall of the Assembly Rooms at Hull, and subsequently examined witnesses at the Hull Infirmary, and also in London. All witnesses who appeared before us were examined on oath. Depositions were read over and signed.

The Board of Trade Inquiry at Hull; the (Vice) 'Admiral' of the Box Fleet under examination (Daily Graphic, 16 Nov. 1904)

Witnesses at the Inquiry.

A Russian representative, in the person of the RUSSIAN VICE-CONSUL at Hull, appeared before us, and cross examined witnesses during the morning of the first day of the Inquiry. After the mid-day adjournment, Dr. HERBERT WOODHOUSE, Solicitor, instructed by the Russian Embassy, appeared on its behalf, and cross-examined such witnesses as he saw fit. Every facility was given to him.

We decided that the Inquiry should be divided into two parts, viz: one dealing with the occurrences on the night of the 21st-22nd October, and the other with the injury to persons and damages to property and trade.

We considered it advisable to proceed first with the Inquiry into the former, whilst the events of the night were still fresh in the memory of those who were able to give information concerning them.

It is right that we should here express our high appreciation of the zealous and able manner in which the Hon. Noel Farrer has discharged the onerous duties of Secretary to the Commissioners.

The facts as testified to were as follows:

About midnight on the 21st-22nd October, 1904, some 30 steam trawlers of the "Gamecock" fleet, some 12 of Messrs. Leyman

& Co's fleet, two mission hospital steamers, in most respects similar in design to trawlers, and three Gamecock carriers were engaged in their occupation of fishing on a part of the North Sea Fishing ground - in 55° 18' north latitude, and 5° east longitude, about 200 miles E. by N. of 'the Spurn' in a depth of water of about 23 fathoms ; and some five or six miles to the southward and eastward of a mark-boat, in this case a sailing smack, which it is the practice to anchor in the neighbourhood of the place where the trawling is carried on.

In appearance the craft of the different classes are much alike. The carriers are of somewhat greater size than trawlers and have the bridge abaft the funnel, as also has the trawler "Oceanic".

The particular part of the fishing ground used by these vessels on the night in question is one which has been habitually frequented by trawlers for many years. The "Gamecock" fleet has been in the habit of going to it to trawl for about ten years; and there is evidence to show that it has been frequented for the purpose for at least twenty-five years.

The carriers, whose main business is to take the fish to the market in the port of London, and the mission-hospital vessels also trawl when not otherwise occupied. On the night in question they were working with their trawls.

On the night in question - which was less than three days before full moon - the weather was hazy with occasional "Scotch mist", but it cleared from time to time, and until between 6 and 8am, was seldom 'thick' or such as to prevent a ship's light being seen at a considerable distance.

All the vessels above mentioned, whether trawlers, carriers or mission-hospital ships, carried and showed the regulation lights. Each carried and showed a 'stern light' in the after part; and in the 'fish pound', or inclosure of boards on the upper deck, many had burning two, in some cases three, bright paraffin lights to enable the hands gutting and sorting the fish to see how to do their work. The fleet works under the direction of an Admiral or Vice-Admiral, and on the night in question was working under the direction of the Vice-Admiral. The Vice-Admiral's vessel carried and showed, in addition, two 'Admiral's lights'. Most of the trawlers were heading about E.N.E., with the wind, which was about S.S.E. and moderate, on their starboard sides. A few on the outskirts of the fleet were heading in different directions.

MR A.M. JACKSON (representing the company) produces models showing the position of the trawling gear in relation to the vessels

Andrew M. Jackson, solicitor, representing the trawler owners.

31

All had one sail, the mizzen, set; a few had both main sail and mizzen set. The speed of the vessels trawling was about 2½ knots.

Every vessel had a capital letter and a number painted in plain figures on her bows, and other distinctive marks abaft and on her funnels.

At about midnight rockets had been fired from the mark-boat and the Vice-Admiral's trawler for the purpose of directing the fishing.

The circumstances being as above stated, the lights of several steamers were observed by the trawlers approaching from the northward and eastward. The strangers seemed to be standing directly for the body of the trawling fleet, and as they approached they seemed to port their helms and steer so as to pass outside and to the northward and to leeward of the main body of the fishing fleet. In passing they turned searchlights on to the trawlers and made signals with coloured lights. The vessels were recognised as men-of-war and the signals they used show that they were foreigners and not British. Their number was, according to the evidence, four or five. They will be referred to hereafter as Group (A).

Shortly after they had got near the trawling fleet the lights of a second group, hereafter referred to as (B), were observed by the trawlers also to the northward and eastward, steering apparently directly for the fleet. The vessels of this group seemed to starboard their helms and alter course somewhat to the southward, so that they passed to the southward or to windward of all except a few vessels of the trawling fleet. Groups (A) and (B), except when using helm as above mentioned, were both standing to the southward and westward. A diagram representing the position of the men-of-war and most of the trawlers at the time when the firing commenced, and as it appeared to the witnesses, will be found in the Appendix. The bearings and distances were estimated by the witnesses, not fixed by exact observation.

When Group (B) had come up to and was near the main body of the trawling fleet, the ships comprising this group (about five in number) were observed to be going slow or to have stopped. Both Groups (A) and (B) were showing their ordinary under-way lights and continued to do so. The vessels of Group (B) used searchlights, throwing them on the fishing fleet in all directions, and also made coloured light signals of the same kind as those used by Group (A), thus disclosing their character as men-of-war of a foreign country.

About midnight, one trawler, viz. the "Tomtit" - which was away from the main body of the fleet

J.W. White, skipper of the Mission ship showing metal splinters removed from the wounded men to Sir Cyprian Bridge (left) and Mr Aspinall Q.C (right).

was to the S.S.W. of the Vice-Admiral's trawler, the 'Ruff' - observed lights to the N.N.E.; and also saw two vessels - hereafter referred to as Group (C) - one of which used searchlights, and both of which were much nearer than the lights which the 'Tomtit' had seen to the N.N.E. These vessels - Group (C) as shown by the system of signals they used, were foreign men-of-war.

As regards time it is to be stated that the trawlers' clocks varied.

The two men-of-war - Group (C) - which were to the southward and in advance of the others, passed the 'Tomtit',which was heading to the East, on her port side, that is to say, to the northward and to leeward of her, the wind being about S.S.E.

Both vessels stopped near the trawler. The one which was nearest fired. Shots were seen by the Master of the trawler to strike the water ahead of him. The second of these two men-of-war was not seen to fire. Both these men-of-war - Group (C) - altered course, passed across the "Tomtit's" bows, and one was observed to move off to the southward and westward.

Very shortly after the two ships of Group (C) were sighted by the isolated trawler "Tomtit" and were observed by the latter to be using their searchlights, the ships of Group (B) opened fire. They fired from both sides and in various directions, some of the trawlers being within very short range at the time.

Some of the witnesses spoke of there being two other men-of-war to windward of Group (B) as appears in the diagram, and stated that these vessels also fired, having previously used coloured light signals and worked searchlights.

Two of the fishermen of the trawler "Mino" stated that immediately before the firing of Group (B) commenced, they heard a bugle sound from the leading ship of the group. It was at first thought by the fishermen that the men-of-war were engaged in a sham fight, but they soon discovered their mistake. After the firing began, the Vice-Admiral of the fishing fleet fired green rockets, the trawler "Tomtit" sent up a white rocket. This was done in the hope of stopping the firing.

The trawlers which were already making known their character by showing their proper lights, had no means of signalling to stop the men-of-war from firing on them, and there is no known signal for that purpose.

According to the evidence, the firing lasted from about 10 to 30 minutes; in our opinion it lasted at least 10 minutes. The firing was from guns and small arms, or machine guns using rifle calibre bullets. Some of the witnesses stated that the firing stopped as soon as one of the ships threw the beams of her searchlights up at an angle of about 45 degrees.

It has in our opinion been established by the evidence that amongst the trawlers previously to or on the night in question there were no torpedo boats of any nationality,and in fact, except the visiting British cruiser some weeks before, no strangers of any kind other than the men-of-war above mentioned. It has also been established that in no case had any trawler on board her any person belonging to the service of or employed by the Japanese or any naval war material of any kind.

NORTH SEA INCIDENT

Two witnesses, viz, George Kitchen Green, the skipper of the "Gull" and Edwin Costello, the boatswain of the "Gull", stated that they imagined they each saw a torpedo boat. These craft were, in our opinion, the trawler "Crane", which was sunk by the firing, and the mission ship "Alpha". The "Crane" and the "Alpha" before the firing commenced were showing lights. In consequence of the firing all the lights of the "Crane" save one "pound light" were extinguished, and her mizzen which had been set was brought down by the firing. The "pound light" which was not extinguished was upon the deck of the trawler, and the glass was shattered by the firing. Green, the skipper of the "Gull" stated that the craft which he had imagined was a torpedo boat immediately afterwards showed a white and a red light, that he kept her under continuous observation; that he saw that she in fact was a trawler; that he proceeded towards her; that her crew hailed him that the trawler was sinking; that he sent a boat to her assistance; that she proved to be the trawler "Crane"; and that his boat brought off all the crew. The crew of the "Crane" gave evidence that they had shown a white and a red light for the purpose of getting assistance.

This evidence shows that the dark object which had been thought to be a torpedo boat was in fact the trawler "Crane". It was corroborated by the evidence of Edwin Costello, the boatswain, and of Harry Smirk, the chief engineer of the "Gull".

The "Crane", which before the firing, had been heading the same way as the other trawlers near her, turned off to starboard after the firing had begun and headed towards the ships which fired. This was not until the skipper who had been conning the trawler was killed, her steering gear was damaged by shot, and she was no longer under command.

In consequence of the firing the skipper of the mission ship "Alpha" starboarded his helm so as to bring his vessel's stern towards the warships which were firing upon him, and also extinguished his lights. Edwin Costello the boatswain of the "Gull", stated that the craft, which, after the firing had begun, he had taken for a torpedo-boat, was, in his opinion, the mission ship "Alpha". This, we find, is the fact. The position of the "Alpha" as shown by the evidence of other witnesses, corroborates this.

The beams of the electric searchlights, used by the men-of-war, were so directed that the letters, numbers, marks, and character of the trawlers could, and ought to have been plainly seen. The firing was continued some time after this was the case.

The fragments of projectiles found on board the trawlers which had been hit during the firing, have been identified as those used in the Russian service. The ships which fired on the trawlers, on the night of the 21st-22nd October, belonged to the Russian Navy. In the Appendix will be found details of the character and marking of the projectiles.

We find that as a result of the firing upon the trawlers on the night of the 21st-22nd October, 1904, two men-

George Henry Smith,

William Arthur Leggett

- were killed.

Six men-

William Smith

John Nixon

Harry Hoggart

Arthur Rea

Albert A. Almond

John Ryder

-were wounded, Hoggart's wound being such as to incapacitate him permanently.

One trawler, the "Crane" was sunk. Five other trawlers, the "Mino", the "Moulmein", the "Gull", the "Snipe', the "Majestic", were hit by shot and damaged. Other trawlers, again, were damaged by the effect of shell explosions close to them. In several cases trawling gear was lost or damaged. The trade plied by the "Gamecock" fleet of Messrs. Kelsall Bros. & Beeching, and by the fleet of Messrs. Leyman & Co - which trade is a matter of careful organisation - was disorganised and rendered unproductive for a time.

The total amount of the damage cannot yet be ascertained, the owners of the trawlers, wherever possible, keeping their vessels at work, so as to avoid further disorganisation and consequent increase of expense. The exact amount of damage done to persons, property, and trade, and the claims for compensation will be made the subject of the further report which we propose to render when all the claims have been presented and considered.

Walter Lumb, the mate of the trawler "Oceanic" states that after the firing ceased one of the warships remained in the vicinity for about half an hour.

According to the evidence of men on board the trawler "Kennet", a warship passed them during daylight at about 7 or 7.15am on October 22nd, and fired at their trawler. The hull of this vessel was black; she had two funnels - the foremost funnel all black, the after funnel a lightish colour and black at the top; two masts, with two yards on each mast; and there were 30 or 40 bluejackets on her forecastle deck. She stopped for about three or four minutes, and then steamed away to the S.S.W.

We wish to make special mention of the bravery and coolness shown by Charles Beer, Harry Smirk, and Edwin Costello of the "Gull" in attempting to save the "Crane" and in assisting to get her dead and wounded crew over to the "Gull."

We further wish to submit for consideration the conspicuous gallantry shown by William Smith, mate of the "Crane", and Arthur Rea, second engineer of the same trawler. Both of these men were wounded. Smith, who was still in bed during our visit to Hull, in spite of his wound assisted Hoggart, rendered helpless by his hand being shot off, into the "Gull's" boat and then refused to leave the sinking "Crane" till every one of the crew had got into the boat, because, being the mate and his skipper being killed, it was his duty to remain on board and be the last to leave his ship.

Arthur Rea, second engineer, also wounded, when he found the water coming into the "Crane", put an extra feed on to the boiler, and partially drew the fires under it. He went a second time, whilst the ship was sinking, to the engine room which was in darkness, the lights having been extinguished by the firing, and stopped the engines, thereby rendering possible the saving of the lives of the crew.

In reporting, as directed, on the case generally, we find that at the time in question a number of British trawlers were peacefully engaged in the pursuit of a lawful calling on a well-known fishing ground in the North Sea: and that there was violent interruption of a customary and properly conducted operation of trade at a spot out of the way of the ordinary course of ships passing between the Skaw and the Straits of Dover, and in no sense in the vicinity of the theatre of current hostilities or of the immediate approaches thereto. There was no person employed by or on behalf of any foreign government, and there was no article of war material belonging to a belligerent or to anyone else on board any of the craft in the trawling fleet, each one of which was conspicuously displaying the lights and numbering enjoined by the regulations issued in accordance with international conventions. The Board of Trade Regulations for Preventing Collisions at Sea which contain, amongst others, the rules concerning lights to be carried by trawlers, are attached hereto, and form part of our report. All these trawlers had at least one sail set.

We find that these trawlers were without warning or provocation fired upon (many at short range) by several men-of-war belonging to Russia; that the firing continued after the electric searchlights of the firing ships had been turned on the trawlers long enough to have made it easy to distinguish their character as peaceful fishing craft. The firing, which as we have said was without warning, was continued deliberately; at least ten minutes, and was on the evidence before us without reason or justification.

We also find that none of the Russian men-of-war after they had ceased to fire on the vessels of the trawling fleet took steps to render any assistance to, or to ascertain the condition of, the craft and crews on which they had been firing: and that there would have been a more serious loss of life, amounting at least to the whole of the wounded belonging to the sunken trawler "Crane", had not three of the crew of the "Gull" with great coolness and gallantry gone to their assistance.

We think that all the evidence of the men present in the trawling fleet which could throw any light upon this matter has been brought before us. We also are of opinion - having seen and heard the witnesses - that their evidence was honest, truthful, and accurate.

We have the honour to be, Sir,

Your obedient Servants,

CYPRIAN A.G. BRIDGE

BUTLER ASPINALL

NOEL M. FARRER,
SECRETARY.

12th December, 1904

3 The International Commission

The international commission assembled in Paris and had its first sitting on the 22nd December. There were a number of reports in the British press at the time that Russian agents had been making strenuous efforts to suborn witnesses into making statements supporting the view that torpedo boats were present in the North Sea on that fateful evening. After an adjournment the commission reconvened on the 9th January and the conclusions it reached were as follows: [23]

Report of the Commissioners, drawn up in accordance with Article 6 of the Declaration of St Petersburgh of the 12th (25th) November, 1904.

1   THE Commissioners, after a minute and prolonged examination of the whole of the facts brought to their knowledge in regard to the incident submitted to them for enquiry by the Declaration of St Petersburgh of the 12th (25th) November, 1904, have proceeded to make, in this Report, an analysis of these facts in their logical sequence. By making known the prevailing opinion of the Commission on each important or decisive point of this summary, they consider that they have made sufficiently clear the causes and the consequences of the incident in question, as well as the deductions which are to be drawn from them with regard to the question of responsibility.

2   The second Russian squadron of the Pacific fleet, under the command-in-chief of Vice-Admiral Aide-de-Camp General Rojdestvensky, anchored on 7th (20th) October, 1904, off Cape Skagen, with the purpose of coaling before continuing its voyage to the Far East.

It appears, from the depositions made, that, from the time of the departure of the squadron from the roads of Reval, Admiral Rojdestvensky had had extreme precautions taken by the vessels placed under his orders, in order that they may be fully prepared to meet a night attack by torpedo-boats, either at sea or at anchor.

These precautions seemed to be justified by the number of reports received from the Agents of the Imperial Government on the subject of hostile events to be feared, which in all likelihood would take the form of attacks by torpedo-boats.

Moreover, during his stay at Skagen, Admiral Rojdestvensky had been warned of the presence of suspect vessels on the coast of Norway. He had learned also, from the Commander of the transport 'Bakan'

The North Sea Inquiry Commission, sitting in Paris, June 1905.

coming from the North, that he had seen on the previous night four torpedo-boats, carrying a single light only, and that at the mast head.

This news made the Admiral decide to start twenty-four hours earlier.

3   Consequently, each of the six distinct divisions of the fleet got under way separately in its turn, and reached the North Sea, independently, in the order indicated by Admiral Rojdestvensky's Report, that flag officer commanding in person the last division, formed by the four new battleships 'Prince Souvoroff', 'Emperor Alexander III,' 'Borodino', 'Oriel', and the transport 'Anadyr'.

The division left Skagen on the 7th (20th) October at 10 o' clock in the evening. A speed of 12 knots was ordered for the two first divisions, and of 10 knots for the following divisions.

4   Beteween 1.30 and 5.15 in the afternoon of the next day, the 8th (21st) October, all the divisions of the squadron passed in turn the British steamer 'Zero' , the captain of which examined the different units attentively enough to enable them to be recognised from his description of them.

The results of his observations are, moreover, in general agreement with the statements in Admiral Rojdestvensky's report.

5   The last vessel which passed the 'Zero' was, from his description of her, the 'Kamchatka'. This transport , which originally was in a division with the 'Dmitri Donskoi' and the 'Aurora' , was, therefore, left behind and isolated about 10 miles to

A 3pdr. Quick-firing gun similar to those which fired on the trawlers (The Daily Graphic, 4 November, 1904)

British officials and witnesses posed for the camera at the North Sea Inquiry Commission, Paris, 1905.

the rear of the squadron. She had been obliged to slacken speed in consequence to damage to her engines. This accidental delay was, perhaps, incidentally the cause of the events which followed.

6 Towards 8 o' clock in the evening, this transport did, in fact, meet the Swedish vessel 'Aldebaran' and other unknown vessels and opened fire on them, doubtless in consequence of the anxiety inspired in the circumstances of the moment by her isolation, the damage to her engines, and her small fighting value.

However this may be, the Commander of the 'Kamchatka', at 8.45 o' clock, sent a message by wireless telegraphy to his Commander-in-Chief, regarding this encounter, stating that he was "attacked on all sides by torpedo-boats."

7 In order to understand the effect which this news had on Admiral Rojdestvensky's subsequent decisions, it must be remembered that, in his estimate, the attacking torpedo-boats, of whose presence, 50 miles to the rear of the division which he commanded, he was thus, rightly or wrongly, informed, might overtake and attack him about 1 o' clock in the morning.

This information led Admiral Rojdestvensky to signal to his ships about 10 o' clock in the evening to redouble the vigilance and look out for an attack by torpedo-boats.

8 On board the 'Souvoroff', the Admiral had thought it indispensable that one of the two superior officers of his staff should be on watch on the Captain's bridge during the night in order to observe, in his place, the progress of the squadron, and to warn him at once if any incident ocurred.

On board all the ships, moreover, the standing orders of the Admiral laid down that the officer of the watch was authorised to open fire in case of an evident and imminent attack by torpedo-boats.

If the attack was from the front he was to open fire on his own initiative, and, in the contrary case, which would be much less pressing, he was to refer to his Commanding Officer.

With regard to these orders, the majority of the Commissioners consider that they were in no way excessive in time of war, and particularly in the circumstances, which Admiral Rojdestvensky had every reason to consider very alarming, seeing that it was impossible for him to verify the accuracy of the warnings that he had received from the Agents of his Government.

9 Towards 1 o' clock in the morning of the 9th (22nd) October, 1904, the night was rather dark, a slight low fog partly clouding the air. The moon only showed intermittently through the clouds. A moderate wind blew from the south-east, raising a long swell, which gave the ships a roll of 5 degress on each side.

The course followed by the squadron towards the south-west would have taken the last two divisions, as the event proved, close past the usual fishing ground of the fleet of Hull trawlers, which was composed of some thirty of these small steam boats, and was spread over an area of several miles.

It appears from the concordant testimony of the British witnesses that all these boats carried their proper lights, and were trawling in accordance with their usual rules, under the direction of their 'Admiral' and in obedience to the signals given by the conventional rockets.

10. Judging from the communications received by wireless telegraphy, the divisions which preceded that of Admiral Rojdestvensky across these waters had signalled nothing unusual.

It became known afterwards, in particular, that Admiral Folkersam, having been led to pass round the fishing fleet on the north, threw his electric searchlight on the nearest trawlers at close quarters, and, having seen them to be harmless vessels, quietly continued his voyage.

11. A short time afterwards the last division of the squadron, led by the 'Souvoroff' flying Admiral Rojdestvensky's flag, arrived in its turn close to the spot where the trawlers were fishing.

The direction in which this division was sailing led it nearly towards the main body of the fleet of trawlers, round which and to the south of which it would therefore be obliged to sail, when the attention of the officers of the watch on the bridges of the 'Souvoroff' was attracted by a green rocket, which put them on their guard. This rocket, sent up by the 'Admiral' of the fishing fleet,

indicated in reality, according to regulation, that the trawlers were to trawl on the starboard tack.

Almost immediately after this first alarm, and as shown by the evidence, the look-out men who, from the bridges of the 'Souvoroff', were scanning the horizon with their night glasses, discovered "on the crest of the waves on the starboard bow, at an approximate distance of 18 to 20 cables," a vessel which aroused their suspicions because they saw no light and because she appeared to be bearing down upon them.

When the suspicious-looking vessel was shown up by the searchlight, the look-out men thought they recognised a torpedo-boat proceeding at great speed.

It was on account of these appearances that Admiral Rojdestvensky ordered fire to be opened on this unknown vessel.

The majority of the Commissioners express the opinion, on this subject, that the responsibility for this action and the results of the fire to which the fishing fleet was exposed are to be attributed to Admiral Rojdestvensky.

12. Almost immediately after fire was opened to starboard, the 'Souvoroff' caught sight of a little boat on her bow barring the way, and was obliged to turn sharply to the left to avoid running it down. This boat, however, on being lit up by the searchlight, was seen to be a trawler.

To prevent the fire of the ships being directed against this harmless vessel, the searchlight was immediately thrown up at an angle of 45^0 .

The Admiral then made the signal to the squadron 'not to fire on the trawlers'. But at the same time that the searchlight had lit up this fishing-vessel, according to the evidence of witnesses, the look-out men on board the 'Souvoroff' perceived to port another vessel, which appeared suspicious from the fact of its presenting the same features as were presented by the object of their fire to starboard.

Fire was immediately opened on this second object, and was, therefore, being kept up on both sides of the ship, the line of ships having resumed their original course by a correcting movement without changing speed.

13. According to the standing orders of the fleet, the Admiral indicated the objects against which the fire should be directed by throwing his searchlight upon them; as each vessel swept the horizon in every direction with her own searchlights to avoid being taken by surprise, it was difficult to prevent confusion.

The fire, which lasted from ten to twelve minutes, caused great loss to the trawlers. Two men were killed and six others wounded; the 'Crane' sank; the 'Snipe', the 'Mino', the 'Moulmein', the 'Gull' and the 'Majestic' were more or less damaged.

On the other hand, the cruiser 'Aurora' was hit by several shots. The majority of the Commissioners recognize unanimously that the vessels of the fishing fleet did not commit any hostile act, and the majority of the Commissioners being of opinion that there were no torpedo-boats either among the trawlers nor anywhere near, the opening of fire by Admiral Rojdestvensky was not justifiable.

The Russian Commissioner, not considering himself in sharing this opinion, expresses the conviction that it was precisely the suspicious-looking vessels approaching the squadron with hostile intent which provoked the fire.

14. With reference to the real objectives of this nocturnal firing, the fact that the 'Aurora' was hit by several 47 millim. and 75 millim. shells would lead to the supposition that this cruiser, and perhaps even some other

Alfred Cosier Fletcher, (died at sea 1941, aged 59) skipper of the Amarapoora, one of the witnesses at the Paris Inquiry.

Russian vessels, left behind on the route followed by the 'Souvoroff', unknown to that vessel, might have provoked and been the object of the first few shots. This mistake might have been caused by the fact that this vessel, seen from astern, was apparently showing no light, and by a nocturnal optical illusion which deceived the look-out on the flagship.

On this head, the Commissioners find that they are without important information which would enable them to determine the reasons why the fire on the port side was continued.

According to their conjecture, certain distant trawlers might have been mistaken for the original objectives, and thus fired on directly. Others, on the contrary, might have been struck by a fire directed against more distant objectives. These considerations, moreover, are not in contradiction with the impressions formed by certain of the trawlers, who, finding that they were struck with projectiles and remained under the rays of the searchlights, might believe that they were the objectives of a direct fire.

15 The time during which the firing lasted on the starboard side, even taking the point of view of the Russian version, seems to the majority of the Commissioners to have been longer than necessary. But the majority consider that, as has already been said, they have not before them sufficient data as to why the fire on the port side was continued. In any case, the Commissioners take pleasure in recognising, unanimously, that Admiral Rojdestvensky personally did everything he could, from beginning to end of the incident, to prevent trawlers, recognised as such, from being fired upon by the squadron.

16 Finally, the 'Dmitri Donskoi', having signalled her number, the Admiral decided to give the general signal for 'cease firing'. The line of his ships then continued on their way, and disappeared to the south-west without having stopped. On this point, the Commissioners recognise, unanimously, that after the circumstances which preceded the incident and those who produced it, there was, at the cessation of fire, sufficient uncertainty with regard to the danger to which the division of vessels was exposed to induce the Admiral to proceed on their way.

Nevertheless, the majority of the Commissioners regret that Admiral Rojdestvensky, in passing the Straits of Dover, did not take care to inform the authorities of the neighbouring Maritime Powers that, as he had been led to open fire near a group of trawlers, these boats, of unknown nationality, stood in need of assistance.

17 In concluding this Report, the Commissioners declare that their findings, which are theirin formulated, are not, in their opinion, of a nature to cast any discredit upon the military qualities or the humanity of Admiral Rojdestvensky, or of the personnel of his squadron.

4 Aftermath and Conclusions

The Russians were held liable for compensation of £65,000, which was in fact £5000 more than the assessment by Board of Trade officials in Britain, who had trimmed down the original claims of the injured parties totalling £100,000. There is no doubt that from a very early stage, despite public indignation and a strong speech by the prime minister, the government, through foreign office diplomats, were adopting a conciliatory approach to the Russians. There was no attempt to press the moral advantage and extract the maximum compensation and the profoundest expressions of regret. It is clear that the British ministers were mindful of the very shaky condition of the Russian state at the time, with widespread disorder and dissatisfaction with the Tsarist regime. They had no wish to do anything which might contribute to the fall of the monarchy, an event which would have had dire results for the stability of Europe and the balance between the contending Imperial powers. Early in January 1905, whilst the North Sea Commission was sitting, there were strikes and violent confrontations in St Petersburg and a gathering in front of the Winter Palace was dispersed with great bloodshed [24]. At Sebastopol in the Crimea the naval depots were destroyed by sailors of the Black Sea fleet, and early in February the Grand Duke Sergei was assassinated by a bomb thrown into his carriage whilst riding through the streets of Moscow.

The *Hull Daily Mail* for 15 March 1905 commented as follows:

'Those who have suffered, naturally feel that the sum agreed was totally inadequate; having regard to the rare and peculiar circumstances involved. The actual amounts claimed, the exact apportionments will not probably be known until the British government issue the promised paper containing this interesting information.

It is understood. however. that the original total claim was about £100,000, so that roughly speaking about two-thirds of the sum has been allowed, the British assessors deducting the other third so as to bring the compensation figure to an amount they could reasonably demand and defend.

All the claims it is assumed will be settled on this basis, viz. two thirds of the amount asked for. Mrs Smith, the widow of the skipper of the *Crane,* has been awarded £5,000, 'an amount which if properly invested will yield between £3 and £4 a week.'

The primary award in each case being supplemented by a sum to cover clothes and belongings lost in the attack. The parents of Leggett received between £800 and £1,000, and the Mission to Deep Sea Fishermen £3,906 for repairs to the *Alpha*. Others received small sums and the balance went to the Gamecock fleet for damage to their vessels and loss of income. Even the smaller payments were huge windfalls to humble fishermen, and Walter Wood, writing in 1911 said:

"The receipt of these considerable sums of money by men who had not been accustomed to

NORTH SEA INCIDENT

The original claims with the assessment of the Board were as follows: [25]

Class	Nature of Claim	Amount Claimed £	s.	d.	Amount Assessed £	s.	d.
I	Loss or death of relative	10,670.	0.	0.	5,800.	0.	0.
II	Wounds by gunfire	17,472.	0.	0.	6,700.	0.	0.
III	Personal injuries directly due to gunfire	310.	0.	0.	137.	0.	0.
IV	Loss of clothes and other effects (including incidental expenses in one instance)	177.	9.	6.	177.	9.	6.
V	Loss of earnings and wages due to detention, absence of ship from fishing ground for repair, etc.	362.	0.	0.	172.	6.	0.
VI	Physical indisposition after exposure to unusual danger and loss of earning power due to shock	1,100.	0.	0.	1,100.	0.	0.
VII	Saving life and property	2,500.	0.	0.	650.	0.	0.
VIII	Complete loss of vessel and consequent loss of her earnings	8,342.	18.	8.	6,834.	18.	8.
IX	Examination and repair of vessels damaged by reason of the firing	10.351.	10.	0.	9,141.	0.	0.
X	Loss of fishing gear	646.	6.	6.	646.	6.	6.
XI	Demurrage whilst vessels were detained in harbour for examination, repairs etc.	7,552.	0.	0.	5,676.	0.	0.
XII	Loss of and disturbed fishing, 21st and 22nd October 1904, and following days loss of rebate etc.	2,458.	9.	8.	2,202.	9.	8.
XIII	Diminution in catch						
XIV	Loss on sales						
XV	Loss of freight	38,476.	0.	0.	17,779.	10.	0.
XVI	Loss of services of skipper killed						
XVII	Increased management expenses due to unprecedented nature of the incident						
XVIII	Surveyors fees and miscellaneous expenses due to the incident	1,319.	16.	4.	915.	6.	4.
		101,748.	10.	8.	57,942.	6.	8.
	Costs of solicitors and accountants	2,081.	12.	5.	2,081	12.	5.
	TOTAL	103,830.	3.	1.	60,023.	19.	1.

the control of such large amounts proved far from an unmixed blessing, and in one or two cases the compensation allowances were recklessly squandered." [26]

The conclusions of the North Sea Commission were a 'fudge', in as much as Admiral Rozhestvensky, whilst being held totally responsible for initiating the action, was also said to have done everything possible to prevent any trawler identified as such being fired upon. The state of near panic in the Russian fleet leading up to the incident seems to have been accepted without demur, with the implication that hostile torpedo boats were to be expected in the North Sea. Whilst regretting that the Admiral did not inform the British or other authorities that assistance was required by the stricken vessels, the report concluded by absolving both him and his officers of any action descreditable to their 'military qualities or humanity'.

The second Pacific Squadron steamed on through the English Channel leaving the people of Hull to mourn their dead and the politicians to avert a possible war.

The fleet was divided at Tangiers - the smaller and older vessels (*Sissoi Veliky, Navarin*, three light cruisers and the destroyers) went the shortest route through the Suez Canal, while Rozhestvensky took the majority of the force round the Cape. There was still considered to be the possibility of an attack from units of the Japanese navy, as well as being wary of any aggressive action by the British. Splitting the force would help confuse any such plans and also give more time for the crews to develop their seamanship.

Payment made to individual fishermen included the following:	
William Smith, mate of the *Crane*	£2,000
additional sum for clothing	£18
John Ryder, deck hand of the *Crane*	£1,500
additional sum for clothing	£12
John Nixon, chief engineer	£500
additional sum for clothing	£16. 5. 0.
Arthur Rea, second engineer	£400
additional sum for clothing	£16. 10 .0.
Albert Almond, trimmer	£300
additional sum for clothing	£19. 1. 9.

In the elaborate political manoeuvring that marked out the relations between the Imperial powers, the German Emperor attempted to use the North Sea Incident as a means of creating a new alliance between Germany and Russia. These overtures were ignored by the Tsar, even though the established Russian-French alliance had been undermined by the Entente Cordiale between Britain and France. The Russian fleet, sailing around Africa and later along the shores of French Indo-China, were to encounter many difficulties dealing with the French colonial administrators when seeking water, provisions and facilities for coaling. Response to the arrival of the Russian armada was often ambiguous, a confused reaction of traditional support and an attempt to follow the public policy of the French government in support of the British. Many once-remote colonial outposts were now linked by the telegraph system, which transmitted through submarine cables news and political commands from Europe within hours or days rather than weeks

THE MAN OFFICIALLY RESPONSIBLE FOR THE DOGGER BANK OUTRAGE.
Admiral Rojdestvensky, who commanded the Baltic Squadron.

Admiral Rozhestvensky (1848-1909); Vice Admiral of the Russian Navy.

Admiral Togo (1847-1934).

or months. It was harder now to claim ignorance and turn a blind eye, especially with the ever present likelihood of any cooperation being observed by a patrolling British vessel with consequent reports back home and inevitable diplomatic embarrassment.

The Russian fleet was kept supplied with coal mainly through the system of ships and depots of Hamburg-Amerika, the German liner company. This arrangement, though on a commercial basis, was surely part of the Kaiser's attempts to establish a new relationship with the Russians and split them from the French.

The two sections of the Russian fleet rendezvoused in Madagascar, where they reprovisioned and took on coal. It was here also that on the 20 December they received news of the imminent fall of Port Arthur, which finally surrendered on 2 January 1905. There is no doubt that this event helped to mute the feelings of anger and bitterness felt in Britain towards Russia and the actions of its fleet. It was generally considered they had received their just punishment and certainly Admiral Rozhestvensky now found himself in a grave predicament. The Second Pacific Squadron had been despatched to reinforce the Far East fleet, most of which had now been lost, bottled up in the harbour at Port Arthur by the blockading tactics of Admiral Togo, the Japanese naval commander. Instead of being reinforcements they now found themselves the only effective Russian naval force within striking distance of Japan. Unwillingly the fleet remained in Madagascar, awaiting the arrival of the Third Pacific Squadron, a scratch force hastily assembled at Libau (Lepaya). The long wait

An impression of the attack by local artist W.D. Penny, signed and dated 1904; H133, Snipe in the foreground. (Reproduced by permission of Patrick Thirsk.)

Porcelain figures of the 'Fishermen's monument' (Chris Ketchell collection).

Obverse of Albert Medal (bronze ,second class) of Edwin Costello ,bosun of the s.t. Seagull.

Reverse of Albert Medal with inscription recording the assistance Costello gave to the crew of the s.t. Crane.

Brass token for plaice used by the Hull Steam Fishing and Ice Co., the 'Red Cross fleet'

Japanese wood block print with scene from the Russo-Japanese war at Port Arthur; by the artist Nobukazu (1872-1944), published by Hasegawa, 1904.

Wood block print of a parade celebrating the efforts of the Japanese fleet against the Russians at Port Arthur; by the artist Kokyo~and published by Matsuki ,1904.

A. Medal of member of the R.A.O.B. ,the 'Buffaloes' ,a friendly society which organised the fund-raising for the the fishermen's statue.

was not helpful to the Russian cause, for in the meantime the Japanese fleet, weary after months at sea maintaining a blockade were given vital breathing space for maintenance and time to replenish their stores and ammunition. By February they were refreshed and ready for action again, although no major overhauls were possible in this brief span. For the Russians the effects of boredom and homesickness resulted in a number of suicides, and tropical diseases accounted for many other casualties, dead and disabled. There were outbreaks of mutiny aboard several units of the fleet and attempts to improve standards of shooting were hampered by a shortage of ammunition. A long-awaited store ship arrived, not with the expected 12-in. and 6-in. shells but 12,000 pairs of boots and fur-lined winter coats! Practice shooting when it was possible, was so bad that the only hit was made not on the target but on the cruiser *Dmitri Donskoi*! The fleet finally departed from Madagascar on the 16 March 1905 and on the 9 May made contact with the Third Pacific Squadron under Rear-Admiral Nebogatov in Camranh Bay, the great natural harbour on the coast of Vietnam. [27]

This was an impressive piece of sailing by the long-awaited reinforcements, a ramshackle collection of coastal defence vessels and other ancient and obsolescent craft which Rohestvensky had rejected when forming his own squadron.

A few days after the two fleets met up, the *Hull*

The Russian fleet in the Straits of Malacca, (the channel between Malaysia and Sumatra.)

Daily Mail was reporting the award of the Albert Medal to the fishermen of the trawlers *Crane* and *Gull*. [28] Arthur Rea, who whilst the ship was obviously sinking had gone below to stop the engines, and William Smith, the last man to leave the ship, were both given the first-class award. Henry Smith, Charles Beer and Edwin Costello, all of the *Gull,* were given the Albert Medal second class. They were received by His Majesty King Edward VII at Buckingham Palace at noon on the 13 May, all except Edwin Costello, who had gone back to Ireland to visit his family. Tragically, on the same day the death was announced of Walter Whelpton, skipper of the *Mino*. He had never been fit enough to return to sea after the shock of the events of that October night in 1904 and he was the third victim to die as a result of the attack. [29]

Meantime, the Russian fleet was heading towards a decisive encounter with the Japanese. On paper there was an apparent balance between the numbers and firepower of the two sides and maybe even a slight advantage in favour of the Russians, but in reality the latter were ill-equipped for such a contest. Saddled with too many antiquated ships and with a

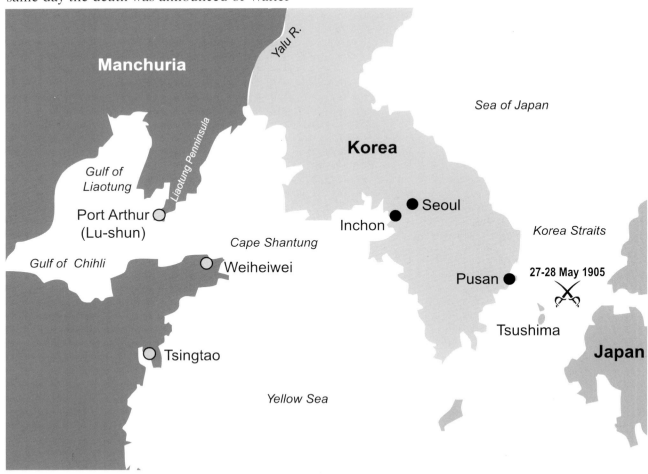

shortage of ammunition, Admiral Rozhestvensky had been at sea for no less than eight months and all were weary and desperate to see their homes once more. In contrast, they were to meet a force refreshed and buoyant after taking part in a great victory, and the men confident in the skill of their leader Admiral Togo, whose well-drilled crews serving a modern fleet were battle-hardened and ready for action.

The two fleets made their fatal encounter in the Korea Straits in a narrow channel between the island of Tsushima and the Japanese mainland; to reach there, the Russians had covered more than 18,000 miles in 224 days. Opening shots were fired at midday on the 27 May 1905 and the battle raged for nearly twenty-four hours.

Action, when it finally came after such a long and morale-sapping journey, seems to have brought out the best in the Russian crews, and their gunners turned out to be a far better than anyone had anticipated. The result, considering all their handicaps, was, however, inevitable and they were comprehensively beaten by the superior naval tactics of the Japanese. Two-thirds of the entire fleet was sunk and a further six vessels were captured. Six others took refuge in neutral ports and four reached the Russian port of Vladivostok. [30] Admiral Rozhestvensky, who had been removed from his sinking flagship unconscious with a fractured skull, was taken to Japan for treatment and eventually allowed to return home, where he died four years later on the 14 January 1909.

The Russo-Japanese war of 1904-1905 resulted in an immense loss of life, though is now largely forgotten in Europe. The Anglo-Japanese alliance, signed in 1902, was a treaty of great value to the Japanese during her war with Russia. In August 1905 the alliance was renewed and extended, and in 1911 renewed for a further ten years a period which included the duration of the Great War. The victory at Port Arthur and the alliance gave Japan its hegemony in China and Korea, which lasted until the 1939-45 war. Defeat for the Russians hastened a process which resulted in revolution and the end of Tsarist rule. On 22 January 1905, three weeks after the surrender of Port Arthur, a protest in St Petersburg led to the massacre of Bloody Sunday, outside the Winter Palace.

Here some 1200 people - men and women- were killed during a large-scale but peaceful attempt to deliver a petition. On 17 February Grand Duke Sergei Alexandrovitch, a stern advocate of autocracy, was killed by a bomb in Moscow.

Belated reforms offered by the Tsar were followed by mutiny on board the *Potemkin* and there was continuing discord until the disastrous mismanagement of Russian involvement in the Great War resulted in the abdication of Tsar Nicholas II, 16 March 1917. This was the end of the Russian monarchy and of the Romanov dynasty founded in 1613 by Michael I.

The final chapter in the story for the people of Hull was enacted in August 1906 with the erection of a memorial to the victims of the Russian Outrage. The suggestion for such a monument had apparently come from Mr F. Hellyer, of the well-known trawler-owning family, and the previous November a committee was elected from the members of the Blythe Boys' Lodge of the RAOB, of which Skipper Smith had been a member, to raise funds for the project. The first subscribers were C.H.Wilson £5, Councillor G.J.Bentham £1.1.0d., J.Watt Esq £5, a 'fishermen's friend' £1.1.0d. and the *Hull Daily Mail* and *Hull Times* also one guinea. The hon. secretary and treasurer of the committee was Alfred Silk, who had been a neighbour of the dead skipper.

The unveiling should have been carried out by Lord Nunburnholme, (Charles Henry Wilson), but he was indisposed and on the morning of the ceremony he asked John Watt JP to take his place. Perhaps surprisingly, considering the initial public reaction to the attack and the considerable sums of money received in compensation, the fund still required a further £60 to meet the full cost of the memorial. The completion of the project had also been delayed by a general election and negotiations for a suitable site with the parks and works committee.

It is clear that the past criticisms of his reaction to the North Sea incident still rankled with Lord Nunburnholme, and the telegram he sent from his home at Warter Priory to Mr Watt repeats the arguments he had made in his earlier rebuttal:

'Very many thanks; will you express my regret at not attending, as it is a unique case of working men showing laudable sympathy with one of their members and it is in no way antagonistic to Russia, with whom we have such large commercial interests; and this deplorable incident can only be looked upon as a terrible

blunder, and these views I expressed at the time and since in the House of Lords to which they assented.

I am sure Sir Seymour King will have no sympathy with the ill-natured correspondence published by the Daily Mail. My family interests in the orphans and fishermen is of 40 years' standing and I wish I had been able to be present today. NUNBURNHOLME' [31]

This was certainly no 'diplomatic' illness, and three years later he died and was buried in the grounds of his home at Warter Priory, E. Yorks. The fishermen's statue was unveiled on the 30 August to the strains of the band of the *Southampton*, the training ship for boys anchored off Sammy's Point. The guests were T.R. Ferens MP and Mrs Ferens; Alderman and Mrs Jarman; Ald. Cohen; Councillors Gould, W. Hakes and T.G. Hall; Mr Chidley ex governor of Hedon Road Jail; Mr and Mrs H.Best; and Mr J Cullen, chairman of the memorial committee representing the RAOB along with Alfred Silk, the Hon. Secretary. Apologies were received from Sir H.Seymour King MP, Sir John Sherburn, Ald. Holder, Councillor Bentham, the Town Clerk, Hon. C.H.Wellesley Wilson MP, the Mayor, Sheriff and Mr Wilson Marsh, all-England secretary of the RAOB.

The memorial still stands, not only as a reminder of the events of 1904 but also of the large fishing community which once inhabited the Hessle Road. Sadly, the fishermen and their families are now dispersed by redevelopment and their numbers greatly reduced by the dramatic decline of the Hull fleet since 1975.

5 Postscript

A transcript of a letter from a Miss Harvard in Canada to her cousin in Hull gives us a glimpse of public reaction overseas. Miss Harvard evidently believed that the Russian Admiral had to have been drunk to perpetrate such an outrage!

'372 Brunswick Ave., Toronto, Nov. 3/04

Dear Cousin Edith,

Your bright and brief epistle reached me on October 29th, and has come across the Atlantic in eight days. We are grieved to hear of our Uncle Alf's sad end, and would express, as far as words can, our sincere sympathy for those who are left. We are also sorry for the two Hull families who were victims of that vodka-soaked Russian admiral; Rojestvensky (sic). May the day soon come when he, and his whole fleet, shall be sent to Davy Jones' locker.

Doubtless, quiet little Hull is in a state of intense excitement. Well, I don't wonder. We would be excited if the Yankees, for instance, took the lives of any of our fishermen. There'd be quite a dust, I can tell you.

I envy you your pleasant situation. Please don't describe that kitchen-window view you have there; it makes my teeth water. I am working in Pa's office at present, but hope, in a year or two, to leave city life and be a farmer. Yes, that's my ambition - to be a farmer. No smoke and grime and noise and worry like there is here in the heart of the city.

No, the country for me. Please don't run yourself down by referring to your photo as 'ugly'. Why, you look a good sight more natural than some photos I've seen. Some people, when sitting for a photo, put on a sweet, cherubic smile, assume a romantic posture, and look altogether as sweet as a cat digesting a bird.

But, say for defiance, insolence, and all the other 'naughtinesses' combined, look at my latest photo which I am mailing you. What a tragic air!

We are having delightful Autumn weather here now, with just a hint of frost at night. The maples and other trees are one blaze of color, and wonderful crops have been gathered all over the Dominion. I am enclosing five of my own little photos: two were taken at the big fire we had, another shows a back view of our house, the fourth is a snap-shot of a balloon ascension, while the fifth shows St. Alban's Cathedral,an Anglican church near our house.

The little caricature you sent, entitled 'E. Mason, the Housemaid' is very cleverly drawn. Send some more please .

Well, as everything has its end, including this letter, I must stop here. In closing, kindest regards are sent to you all (speshully U) by Your Canadian Cousin,

F.B. Harvard

P.S. I am mailing Grandma a half-a-dozen numbers of 'Collier's Weekly' which you can see next time you visit her. There are some real good war photos in them. F.B.H.'*

* These would be of the Russo-Japanese war and the siege of Port Arthur.

A postcard of the damaged trawlers in the Hull fish dock was sent from Hull to someone in Louth, Lincs soon after the funeral of the fishermen:

'Dear Alice

I was very pleased to hear your mother was a little better; give her my love and tell her I hope she will soon be well again. Hope you are well. What do you think to this, it was a bit off was it not, I went to the funeral of the two men who were killed on these ships, it was a great sight, there were three bands and hundreds of people following, Councillors, Aldermen, the Mayor, the men of war from H.M.S. *Hearty*, the streets were lined with people to see it pass.

With love from yours, Jenny'

Huge numbers of postcards were published commemorating the 'Russian Outrage' showing the damaged vessels in dock, the funeral procession, grave site and artists' impressions of the attack in the North Sea.

THE RUSSIAN OUTRAGE.—The 'Moulmein' and 'Mino' in Hull Dock.

THE RUSSIAN OUTRAGE.—The "X" shew shot holes in the bow of the 'Moulmein, and of the 'Mino' Foc'sle.

RUSSIAN OUTRAGE ON HULL TRAWLERS. SCENE AT ST ANDREWS DOCK HULL. S.R & C° BHAM

6 The City of Hull and Tsarist Russia

Hull has had a long history of trade with Scandinavia, Russia and the Baltic states which dates back to the Middle Ages and the Hansa. In the nineteenth century the fortunes of both of the city's premier steamship companies, Bailey and Leetham and the Wilson Line, were intimately linked with northern Europe. Wilson's eventually absorbed their rivals in 1903 and came to an accommodation with their fierce rivals in Denmark, D.F.D.S. Many thousands of economic migrants and Jewish refugees from the Tsarist pogroms were brought to Hull in Wilson's ships, most of them taking the train journey to Liverpool, where they took ship for a new life in the U.S.A.

In 1871 the former chief constructor to the Admiralty, Sir Edward James Reed (1830-1896), became chairman and managing director of Earle's Shipbuilding and Engineering Co. Ltd of Hull. His contacts with governments and naval personnel around the world brought the yard a rich crop of contracts to build a variety of warships for Turkey, Japan, Germany, Chile and Brazil. An order was also received to build a steam yacht for the Tsarevich, Grand Duke Alexander Alexandrovitch. Designed by Reed the launch was witnessed by the Tsarevich who came to Hull on the 4 July 1873 following his unofficial visit to the capital to be a guest at the reception of the Shah of Persia. Received at Paragon station by Sir William Wright, chairman of the Hull Dock Company, Sir E.J. Reed and the civic heads, he was saluted by a guard of honour provided by the East Yorkshire Artillery Volunteers.

In the company of General Zenovieff, General Sturler, Admiral Likatchoff (the Russian naval agent in Britain), Count Alsouvioff, and Capt Raguly, who was to captain the yacht, the imperial party proceeded to the shipyard. Here the Tsarevich made a selection of carpets, curtains, upholstery and furniture for the interior fitting of his vessel and saw the remarkable, but ill-fated, *Bessemer,* then under construction at the yard. This huge, ungainly two-ended, cross-channel steamer was withdrawn from service after only a few weeks operation.

The Russian heir was driven down the Anlaby Road for dinner at Kirkella House, the home of Sr Edward Reed. A brass plaque can still be seen in the master bedroom, which records that 'H.I.M. Alexander III Czar of Russia occupied this room when Czarewitch July 4th to July 7th 1873'.

The launch took place on Saturday the 5 July at about 2pm when to the accompaniment of the Russian national anthem, Miss Reed, daughter of the chairman, christened the 160 ton yacht *Slavyanka*.

His Imperial Highness then embarked on the P.S. *Isle of Axholme*, of the Gainsborough Steam Packet Co, for a short trip on the Humber and inspecting the docks, flying the union flag at the foremast, the Tsarevich's own flag at the main and the Russian standard at the mizzen. The training ship *Southampton*, anchored off the Humber Iron Works (Sammy's Point) was decked overall for the occasion, with the yards manned by the cadets and the ship's band playing the Russian national anthem.

Tying up in the Queen's Dock, opposite the entrance to the wharfage department of the Dock Office (now the Hull Maritime Museum), a carriage waited to drive the royal visitor for luncheon at the Royal Station Hotel.

The yacht was in use during the visit of His Imperial Highness to the Isle of Wight as guest of the Prince and Princess of Wales in August the same year. Daily excursions were the rule, sometimes following the competing yachts during Cowes week. She proved rather small for the considerable number of people who embarked on her, and Reed was invited to Osborne, Queen Victoria and Prince Albert's island 'holiday home,' to receive instructions for building a much more substantial vessel.

The Grand Duke Alexis, brother of the Tsarevich, conveyed a present to Reed of a gold ring with the Tsarevich's initials and crown enriched with diamonds.

On the 1 September 1874, the 800 -ton yacht *Czarevna* was launched by Miss Cissy Reed. Decked with flags, the three-masted, schooner-rigged vessel raised steam soon after entering the water, with Capt Reguly, her master-to-be, looking on.

Elegantly appointed, the saloons were of polished oak, walnut and rosewood, upholstered in velvet and with deckhouses of polished teak. Davits, stanchions and anchor were galvanised iron and she was rigged with galvanised rope. An engine of 130 h.p. by Penn of Greenwich turned a propeller of 11ft 6in diameter to achieve an average speed of 9 to 10 knots. The hull was divided into six watertight sections with two large pumps and suction pipes to all compartments. Five small boats included a steam launch of mahogany by White of Cowes, with a cabin by Earle's. Two complete sets of steering gear were installed on Hastie's patent principle, one of them on top of the deckhouse and the other in the wheelhouse aft. Four small guns were also carried, for signals and salutes.

During trials at the mouth of the Humber, a maximum speed of 14 knots was achieved and the yacht was due to leave for St Petersburg by the end of the year. (Credland 1982)

7 The Men and the Ships

The following names are those fishermen recorded in contemporary newspapers and official reports as being present in the North Sea on the 21-22 October 1904. Those marked by an asterisk were the complement of the *Crane*.

John ALLAN (aged 32),skipper; *Oceanic;* (5 Pretoria Avenue, Edinburgh Street).

* Albert Edward ALMOND (aged 20), trimmer; *Crane*; (unmarried; father at Lowestoft; 2 Tyne Street, Hull)

Charles BEER, mate; *Gull.*

John BROOKE, skipper; *Robin* (a fish carrier).

Thomas CANTWELL, skipper; *Teal.*

Thomas CARR, 'admiral' on the evening of the attack, skipper; *Ruff*. He was actually vice-admiral of the Gamecock fleet, but his senior was ashore.

James Henry CHANDLER, mate; *Burmah.*

Edwin COSTELLO, bosun; *Gull.*

Capt. John Robert DIER, superintendent, Kelsall Bros and Beeching.

William DOUGHTY, bosun; *Mino*; (10 Wilberforce Terrace, Campbell Street).

Alfred EAST, third hand, *Gull.*

Thomas EDMONDS, skipper; *Bassein.*

Walter James EDMONDS, skipper; *Burmah.*

Ralph FALL, skipper; *Avon* (James Leyman and Co.).

Harry FAWCETT, mate; *Mandalay.*

Alfred Cosier FLETCHER, skipper, *Amarapoora.*

John Thomas FLETCHER, skipper; *Swift* (a fish carrier).

Samuel Henry FOOTE, skipper; *Kennett* (Messrs Leyman); 35 years at sea.

James GILLARD, skipper; *Snipe.*

John Charles GILLATT, bosun; *Moulmein.*

John GOWAN, skipper; *Forth*. (James Leyman and Co.).

James GRAY, cook, *Mino;* (9 Norman's Terrace, Campbell Street).

George Kitchen GREEN, skipper; *Gull.*

Charles GUNTON, third hand; *Mino;* (5 Hewson Terrace, Strickland Street).

Thomas HALL, skipper; *Tomtit.*

John Thomas HAMES, skipper; *Moulmein.*

Fred HARTFIELD, mate; *Mino;* (5 Ash Grove, Ash Street). Born in Stettin, Poland.

George HARVEY, second hand; *Dove.*

Herbert HENRY, skipper; *Majestic.*

Christopher HODGSON, skipper, *Cevic.*

* Harry HOGGART (aged 25), bosun; *Crane*; (unmarried; from York but lodged at 102 Manchester Street, Hull).

* Robert JACKSON, mate, *Cevic.*

Bill JOHNSON, bosun; *Rangoon.*

* William Richard LEGGETT (aged 28), second mate (third hand); *Crane;* (unmarried; parents at Gorleston; lodged at 16 Flora Avenue, Carlton Street; other sources give it as Flora's Avenue, Westbourne Street).
His second name is problematic; the Board of Trade Inquiry transcript records it as Arthur, and since his parents gave evidence it would be strange if the name had been entered incorrectly. However both his headstone and the fishermen's memorial statue are inscribed William Richard Leggett.

Walter LUMB, mate; *Oceanic.*

Joseph LYONS, mate; *Kennett* (James Leyman and Co.).

John MARTIN, skipper; *Fame* (the mark boat).

Dr John Wright MASON, Medical Officer of Health and police surgeon, Hull.

Joseph MASON, second hand; *Moulmein.*

Frederick MICHAELSEN, mate (second hand); *Snipe.*

William MITCHELL, mate; *Jed* (James Leyman and Co.)

John MORTIMER, skipper of the Mark Boat *FAME* (43 years experience as a fisherman)

* John NIXON, chief engineer; *Crane*; (from Newcastle; 8 Aberdeen Terrace, West Dock Avenue).

Thomas O'HARA, skipper; *Grouse.*

Matthew PEAKER, skipper; *Magpie* (a fish carrier). Parker had been 49 years a fisherman.

* Arthur REA (aged 22), second engineer; *Crane*; (unmarried; father an engineer, at Earle's shipyard; 42 King St, Charles Street).

* John RYDER, (aged 23) deck hand; *Crane* (unmarried; 117 Longcroft Place, Bradford; elsewhere given as 1 Turk Street, off Chain Street, Bradford.)

William SANDERSON, cook; *Kennett*

William SHUTTLEWORTH, fourth hand; *Mino;* (18 Havelock Street).

Harry SMIRK; chief engineer, *Gull.*

* George Henry SMITH, aged 40, skipper; *Crane;* (married with five children aged 4 to 16; (7 Ribble Avenue, Ribble Street contemporary directories give the house number as 11.)

* Joseph Alfred SMITH (aged 15), cook; *Crane.* (son of the skipper; 7 Ribble Avenue, Ribble Street, Hull.)

* William SMITH (aged 31), mate; *Crane;* (married with three children; 3 Staves Buildings, Porter Street).

James STUBBS, chief engineer; *Mino;* (135 Division Road). Came to Hull from Manchester.

——————— THOMAS, third hand; *Mandalay.*

George William THOMPSON, skipper; *Rangoon.*

Alfred John TUBBY, mate; *Alpha*

John Samuel WATSON, mate; *Knot.*

Walter WHELPTON, skipper; *Mino;* (5 Dee Street). He was born in Gainsborough , Lincs.

John Thomas WHITE, skipper; *Alpha* (mission ship).

Joseph William WHITE, skipper; *Joseph and Sarah Miles*. (Mission ship). Born 1863, son of a missioner of the same name; he was port missioner at Grimsby in 1899 and of Gorleston after leaving the mission ship. Died 13 November 1928.

Other principals:

Butler ASPINALL KC, who with Admiral Bridge was in charge of the Board of Trade inquiry.

Dr Hirjee N. ANKLESARIA, surgeon aboard the mission hospital ship, *Joseph and Sarah Miles*. Graduate of Bombay University, LRCS (Edinburgh).
He is pictured in The Graphic in the sick berth of the mission ship along with an example of a portable X-ray machine. A new invention, the Röntgen machine as it was then called (X-rays having been discovered by Willhelm Conrad Röntgen in 1895, for which he was awarded a Nobel Prize in 1901.)
A similar machine had been taken from the Nikolaevsky hospital in Kronstadt and did valuable service in the Russian fleet at Tsushima, locating hidden shell splinters. This was the first time an X-ray aparatus had been used on a Russian warship in battle (see Tsar's Last Armada, p.296)

George BEECHING, partner in Kelsall Bros and Beeching and managing director of the Gamecock fleet; also fish and ice merchant St Andrew's Dock (home at 121 Coltman Street).

Admiral Sir Cyprian BRIDGE, GCB, director of naval intelligence (1889-94), who with Butler Aspinall KC was in charge of the Board of Trade Inquiry.

Dr Richard Jacob COLMER, surgeon of the mission hospital ship *ALPHA*, which on the evening of 21-22 October was attached to the Gamecock fleet.

Thomas Cathrick JACKSON (1866-1948), solicitor, member of the firm headed by his brother A.M. Jackson. Active in the Royal Yorkshire Yacht Club, of which he was commodore from 1923 until his death. Elected as an honorary brother of Hull Trinity House in 1933.

John KELSALL, principal of Kelsall Bros. and Beeching, trawler owners.

Sir Henry Seymour KING, MP for Central Hull and senior member of H. S. King and Co., East India agents and bankers of London.

The Naval Commanders

Admiral Heihachiro Togo (1847 - 1934)

Trained in England 1871-8, a period which included two years in HMS *Worcester*, a gunnery course on the *Victory* and the study of mathematics at Cambridge. During the Sino-Japanese War, 1894-5, he distinguished himself as captain of the *Naniwa* and was soon after promoted to Admiral. At the outbreak of the Russo-Japanese war he was commander-in-chief of the combined fleet, directed the blockade of Port Arthur (surrendered 2 January 1905) and destroyed the Russian fleet in the Strait of Tsushima 27-8 May 1905.

Greatly admired in the west, he was subsequently the recipient of the British Order of Merit, an outstanding honour for a foreign subject.

Admiral Zinovi Petrovich Rozhestvensky (1848-1909)

Russian naval attaché in London in 1892, he was made a captain in 1895. Commanded Admiral Alexiev's flagship in the Far East during the Sino-Japanese war and then transferred to St Petersburg as head of the gunnery practice squadron of the Baltic fleet until 1902, when he was made Chief of the naval staff, with the rank of rear admiral and aide-de-campe to the Tsar. En route through the North Sea in 1904 he received his commission as vice-admiral and after the defeat at Tsushima he went into retirement and died on the 14 January, 1909.

Vessels in the North Sea fishing grounds 21-22 October 1904.

All of these are mentioned by name in the official reports or in the newspapers, or both.

Mission Hospital Ships, RNMDSF

ALPHA(L0.24) The Mission's first steam hospital ship, steel screw ketch, built 1900 by Hawthorn and Co. Leith, 274 tons, length 135.6 ft, breadth 22.6 ft, depth 13.8 ft. She was sold to Norway in 1926 and renamed *Acta*.
This was the mission vessel officially attached to the Gamecock fleet on October 21st. At the time of the attack, when the fishermen were seeking help they encountered the *Joseph and Sarah Miles* first and the wounded were taken aboard her. The *Alpha* was damaged by several near-misses during the bombardment. She was requisitioned as a minesweeper 1915-1919.

JOSEPH and SARAH MILES (L0.175), steel screw ketch, built 1902, by Hawthorn and Co.

Leith, 272 tons, length 135 ft, breadth 22.5 ft, depth 13.8 ft. The third steam hospital ship; requisitioned as a minesweeper 1915-1919 and used for fisheries research 1920-1921. Scrapped in 1937 after the demise of the 'Box Fleet'.

Trawlers and Carriers

In 1904 Kelsall Bros and Beeching were operating 37 trawlers and 6 carriers in the Gamecock fleet. Thirty-two of these were at the fishing ground at the time of the attack, while the *Bovic* had not reached the main body. In company with them were twelve of the fourteen trawlers of the fleet of James Leyman and Co. (Eton Street, Hull). These latter vessels are characterised by being named after British rivers. All were under command of the Gamecock 'admiral'.

The sudden assault caused trawlers to come to a sudden stop or put on speed to make their escape, both of which resulted in nets being torn or lost as the 'wires' slacked off or came under excessive tension.

All the following are units of the Gamecock fleet, unless otherwise stated:-

AMARAPOORA, (H.59), iron screw ketch, bt. 1895 Edwards Bros, N. Shields, 148 tons, length 100.7 ft, breadth 20.6 ft, depth 11ft. (tore her net.)

(Lost in a collision on the North Sea, 3 May 1912)

AUK (H.755), steel screw ketch, bt. 1903 Goole Shipbuilding and Repairing Co, 168 tons, length 110.0 ft, breadth 21.1 ft, depth 11.1 ft.

AVA, (H.78), iron screw ketch, bt. 1896 ,

Edwards Bros. N. Shields, 162 tons, length 107 ft, breadth 20.6 ft, depth 11.1 ft.

(Lost in the North Sea, 24 February 1910)

AVON, (H.423), steel screw yawl, bt. 1898 Mackie and Thomson, Glasgow, 168 tons, length 105.8 ft, breadth 20.6 ft, depth 11.0 ft. (James Leyman and Co.), (lost her net).

BASSEIN (H.68), iron screw ketch, bt. 1895 Edwards Bros., N. Shields 153 tons, length 105.8 ft., breadth 20.6 ft, depth 11.0 ft,

(Sank in the North Sea, 7 Nov 1911)

BOVIC, (H.51), iron screw ketch, bt. 1896 Edward Brothers, N. Shields, 162 tons, length 107.0 ft, breadth 20.6ft, depth 11.0 ft. (she had apparently not reached the fishing ground at the time of the attack).

(Lost in collision, three miles off Co. Durham, 5 August 1917).

BURMAH, (H.86), iron screw ketch, bt. 1892, Hepple & Co., N. Shields, 168 tons, length 119 ft, breadth 20.6 ft, depth 10.8 ft. (lost her net.)

CEVIC, (H.76), iron screw ketch, bt. 1895, Edwards Bros, N. Shields, 151 tons, length 106 ft, breadth 20.6 ft, depth 11 ft. (lost her net)

CLYDE, (H.425), steel screw yawl, bt. 1898 Mackie and Thomson, Glasgow, 168 tons, length 105.6,ft breadth 21.0 ft, depth 10.7 ft (James Leyman and Co.)

CRANE, (H.756), steel screw ketch, bt. 1903, Goole Shipbuilding and Repairing Co, 168 tons, length 110.3 ft, breadth 20.9 ft, depth 11.1 ft.

She was built at a cost of about £6,000 and was lost the year after entering service.

DON, (H.433), steel screw yawl, bt. 1898, Irvine Shipbuilding, 168 tons, length 105.6 ft, breadth 21.0 ft, depth 10.7 ft (James Leyman and Co)

DOVE, (H.279), iron screw ketch, bt. 1897 Edwards Bros, N. Shields, 168 tons, length 118 ft, breadth 20.7 ft, depth 10.9 ft.

ESK, (H.435), steel screw yawl, bt. 1898, Irvine Shipbuilding, 168 tons, length 105.6 ft, breadth, 21.0 ft, depth 10.7 ft (James Leyman and Co).

FAME, (H.1421), wooden ketch (the Mark Boat) bt. 1884 H. Reynolds, Lowestoft, 75 tons, length 80.4 ft, breadth 20.8 ft, depth 10.6 ft.)

FORTH, (H.469), steel crew yawl, bt. 1899 Irvine Shipbuilding and Engineering Co, 168 tons, length 105 ft, breadth 21 ft, depth 10.7ft (James Leyman and Co)

GOTHIC, (H.67), iron screw ketch, bt. 1895 Edwards Bros, N. Shields, 153 tons, length 105.8 ft, breadth 20.6ft, depth 11.0 ft.

GROUSE, (H.100), iron screw ketch, bt. 1897, Edwards Bros, N. Shields, 167 tons, length 118.3 ft, breadth 20.5 ft,depth 11 ft.

GULL, (H.241), iron screw ketch, bt. 1897, Edwards Bros. N. Shields, 166 tons, length 118.1 ft, breadth 20.5 ft, depth 11 ft.

(Sunk in the North Sea, December 1922)

HULL, (H.473), steel screw ketch, bt. 1899, Mackie and Thomson, Glasgow, 168 tons, length 105.6 ft, breadth 21.0 ft, depth 10.7 ft (James Leyman and Co)

ISIS,(H.474), steel screw ketch, bt. 1899, Mackie and Thomson, Glasgow, 168 tons, length 105.6 ft, breadth, 21.0 ft, depth 10.7 ft (James Leyman Co.)

JED, (H.478), steel screw yawl, bt. 1899 Irvine Shipbuilding and Engineering Co, 167 tons, length 105.6 tons, breadth 21.0 ft, depth 10.7 ft (James Leyman and Co)

KENNETT, (H.480), steel screw yawl, bt. 1899, Irvine Ship-building and Engineering Co, 167 tons, length 105.6 ft, breadth 21 ft, depth 10.7 ft (James Leyman and Co).

KNOT, (H.784), steel screw ketch, bt. 1903, Goole Shipbuilding and Repairing Co, 168 tons, length 110.3, breadth 20.9 ft, depth 11.1 ft.

(Wrecked off Fife Ness, Scotland, 5 November 1916).

LEVEN, (H.489), steel screw ketch, bt. 1900 Mackie and Thomson, Glasgow, 168 tons, length 105.6 ft, breadth, 21.0 ft, depth 10.7 tons (James Leyman and Co.)

MAGPIE, (H.802), (Carrier boat), steel screw ketch, bt. 1904 Goole Shipbuilding and Repairing Co, 278 tons, length 140 ft, breadth 21.6 ft, depth 10.4 ft.

MAJESTIC, (H.181), iron screw ketch, bt. 1891, Cochrane, Cooper and Schofield, Beverley, 152 tons, length 105.4 ft, breadth 20.1 ft, depth 11 ft. (lost nets).

MANDALAY, (H.105), iron screw ketch, bt, 1890, Cook, Welton and Gemmell, Hull, 148 tons, length 103.2, breadth 20.1 ft, depth 11.0 ft.

(Wrecked off Ravenscar, 14 February 1908).

MARTABAN, (H.82), iron screw ketch bt. 1890 by Cook, Welton and Gemmell, Hull, 148 tons, length 103.6 ft, breadth 20.1 ft, 11.0 ft.

MARTIN, (H.187), steel screw ketch (carrier boat) bt. 1897, Edwards Bros, N. Shields, 242

tons, length 133.7 ft, breadth 21.6 ft, depth 10.8 ft.

(Lost 14 April 1917).

MINO (H.799), steel screw ketch, bt 1903, Goole Shipbuilding and Repairing Co, 168 tons, length 110.3 ft, breadth 20.9 ft, dept 11.1 ft.

MOULMEIN, (H.61), iron screw ketch, bt. 1895 Edwards Bros, N. Shields, 151 tons, length 106 ft, breadth 20.6 ft, depth 11 ft.

NIDD, (H.495), steel screw ketch bt. 1900, Mackie and Thomson, Glasgow, 168 tons, length 105.6 ft, breadth 21.0 ft, depth 10.7 ft (James Leyman and Co)

OCEANIC (H.449), iron screw ketch,bt. 1895, T. Charlton, Grimsby, 168 tons, length 102 ft, breadth, 21 ft, depth 11.0 ft. (lost nets).

OUSE, (H.514), steel screw ketch, bt. 1900 Mackie and Thomson, Glasgow, 167 tons, length 104.1 ft, breadth 21.0 ft, depth 10.7 ft (James Leyman and Co.)

OWL, (H.801), steel screw ketch, bt 1904. Goole Shipbuilding and Repairing Co, 169 tons, length 110.3 ft, breadth 21.2 ft, depth 11.2 ft.

PIGEON, (H.155), iron screw ketch, bt 1897 Edwards Brothers, N. Shields, 143 tons, length 106.0 ft, breadth 20.6 ft, depth 10.9 ft.

RANGOON, (H.87), iron screw yawl, bt. 1888 Cook, Welton and Gemmell, Hull, 129 tons, length 100.4 ft, breadth 20.1 ft, depth 10.4 ft (lost net, going at full speed).

ROBIN, (H.4), steel screw ketch, bt. 1904, Goole Shipbuilding and Repairing Co, 169 tons, length 110.3 ft, breadth 21.1 ft, depth 11.2 ft. (lost net).

RUFF, (H.34), steel screw ketch, bt. 1904. Goole Shipbuilding and Repairing Co, 169 tons, length 110.3 ft, breadth 21.1 ft, depth 11.2 ft. (This was the 'Admiral's' boat).

SNIPE, (H.133), iron screw ketch, bt. 1897 Edwards Bros,N.Shields 143 tons, length 106 ft, breadth 20.5 ft, depth 11 ft.

(Sank in the North Sea, 1922)

SWIFT, (H.99), steel screw ketch, (fish carrier) bt. 1897, Edwards Bros, Newcastle, 242 tons, length 133.7 ft, breadth 21.6 ft, depth 10.8 ft (damaged net and gear).

TEAL, (H.90), iron screw ketch, bt. 1897 Edward Bros, N. Shields 143 tons, length 106 ft, breadth 20.5, depth 11.0 ft. (lost net).

(Wrecked off Buckie, Scotland, 2 January 1917)

TEUTONIC, (H.117), iron screw ketch, bt. 1890 Cochranes, Beverley, 152 tons, length 105.4 ft, breadth 20.1 ft, depth 11.0 ft.

(Sank in the North Sea, 25 December, 1906).

THRUSH, (H.703), steel screw ketch, bt. 1902, Goole Shipbuilding and Repairing Co, 166 tons, length 110ft, breadth 21.0 ft, depth 11.1 ft.

TOMTIT (H.35), steel screw ketch, bt. 1897 Edward Bros, N. Shields 143 tons, length 110.3 ft, breadth 21.1 ft, depth 11.2 ft.

WREN, (H.215), iron screw ketch, bt. 1897, Edwards Bros, N. Shields 144 tons, length 118.2 ft, breadth 20.6ft, depth 11.0 ft.

(Sank in North Sea, 18 December 1923).

Back in Hull were the *Britannic, Jay, Paramatta, Prome, Quail, Ibis, Kite, Hawk, Jackdaw* and *Swallow*, also *Greta* and *Mersey* of the Leyman fleet.

The Quail, a Gamecock trawler which was docked in Hull at the time of the attack.

Note:

The trawler *Mino* was sold to the Earl of Kinoull (George Harley Hay) in 1936 when the Gamecock and Red Cross box fleets were put into liquidation. An agreement and crew list dated 23 April 1936 designates her as a steam yacht, with Stanley Todd of Subway Street as skipper. There were nine other crew, all Hull men except the second hand, who was from Yarmouth. Early in 1937 she was fitted out on the Solent to send supplies of food to Spain for refugees of the Civil War but the British government put a stop to the enterprise. As a result the *Mino* was consigned to the breaker's yard at Charleston, North Britain ie. Scotland.

Stanley Todd was a skipper in the Gamecock Fleet and had served in the 1914-1918 war as a gunner in the Royal Field Artillery.

During the 1939-1945 he was a skipper lieutenant in armed trawlers and was involved in the Dunkirk evacuation, as well as the landings at Anzio and Salerno, at the same time as his son was serving in the R.A.F. as an air-gunner. He died in Hull, July 1972.

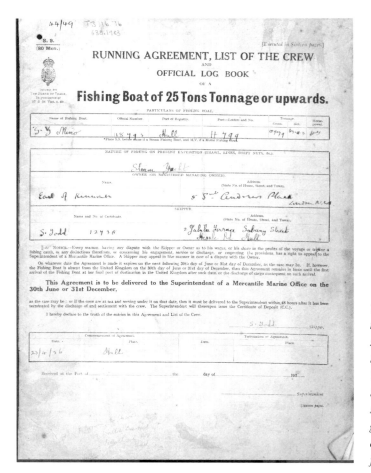

The Mino was sold in 1936 to the Earl of Kinnoulil to send supplies of food to Spain for refugees of the Civil War. Stanley Todd of Subway Street, Hull, was appointed skipper but the British government put a stop to the enterprise and the Mino went for scrap.

8 Memorials and Awards

THE FISHERMEN'S MONUMENT

The monument was placed on the south side of the Hessle Road at the corner of the Boulevard, standing in front of St Barnabas Church. The latter is now demolished, but the statue is still intact. Overall it weighs 16 tons, with a base of Yorkshire stone surmounted by a plinth of red Balmoral granite inscribed :

ERECTED BY PUBLIC SUBSCRIPTION

TO THE MEMORY OF

GEORGE HENRY SMITH

(SKIPPER)

AND

WILLIAM RICHARD LEGGETT

(THIRD HAND)

OF THE ILL-FATED TRAWLER "CRANE"

WHO LOST THEIR LIVES IN THE NORTH SEA

BY THE ACTION OF THE RUSSIAN BALTIC FLEET

OCTOBER 22ND 1904

AND

WALTER WHELPTON

(SKIPPER) OF THE TRAWLER "MINO"

WHO DIED FROM SHOCK MAY 13TH 1905

UNVEILED BY LORD NUNBURNHOLME

AUGUST 30TH 1906

ALBERT LEAKE

SCULPTOR HULL

Above the inscription is the outline of a pair of buffalos horn's and the initials RAOB.

The statue itself is a portrait of Skipper Smith, carved in Sicilian marble, the right hand raised and the left hand holding a pair of binoculars by his side. It has often been said that the figure originally displayed a fish above his head. This is not so, and the story derives from the occasion during the attack when the bosun of the *Tomtit* held up two large fish to demonstrate

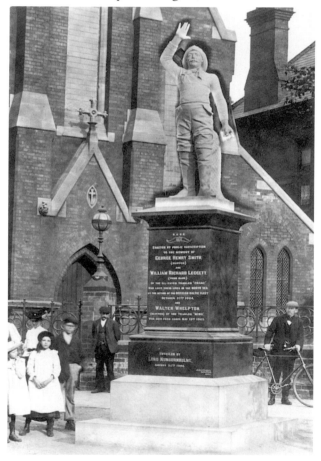

The fishermen's memorial, St Barnabas church behind, at the corner of Boulevard and Hessle Road. Note the buffalo horn symbol of the R.A.O.B. and the name of Lord Nunburnholme carved on the plinth, along with the name of the stonemason, Albert Leake.

Souvenir tissues printed by T. Tather and Sons, 294 Hessle Road, Hull. The second version (below) has the name of John Watt J.P. replacing that of Lord Nunburnholme, who was ill.

to the Russian warships that they were only fishermen about their normal duties.

Albert Leake, stonemason and sculptor of Spring Bank West, was responsible for assembling the monument at a cost of £245. The figure was carved in Italy from a photograph posed by Mr Leake wearing oilskins and a sou'wester (see HDM 5 April 1978). As related abov,e the unveiling was actually performed by John Watt JP, owing to the indisposition of Lord Nunburnholme. T.Tather & Son, printers, 294 Hessle Road, produced souvenirs of the occasion on sheets of tissue, approximately thirteen inches square with an outline illustration of the statue and details of its construction and the words inscribed on the plinth. Also included is a note that 'Ticket-holders assemble at the West Hull Hall, at 2.30, and a procession formed a quarter of an hour later. The Southampton Boys' band will march from the City Square at two o'clock and will play en route. They will also give selections during and after the unveiling ceremony.'

At a later date ornamental models of the monument, each about six inches high, were produced by 'Waterfall Heraldic China', 'Swan China' and other companies producing Goss-type figures. A transfer of the city arms appears on the plinth, sometimes with HULL in a scroll beneath, and below that the legend FISHERMEN'S MONUMENT. The entire inscription is also reproduced on these ornaments.

THE ALBERT MEDAL

The Albert Medal, second class, awarded to Edwin Costello, bosun of the *Gull* was bequeathed to the Hull Museum in 1950 by his sister, Johanna Costello, and forwarded by the Receiver of Wrecks from Blackpool. It is complete with its leather-covered case stamped with the monogram of Edward VII, and the blue and white medal ribbon is still attached. Made in bronze there is the following citation engraved on the reverse:

'Presented by His Majesty to Edwin Costello boatswain of the trawler GULL of Hull for gallantry in rescuing the wounded survivors of the crew of the trawler CRANE when sinking in the North Sea after damage by the gunfire of the Russian fleet on the 21st-22nd October 1904'.

The Albert Medal, first class, given to William Smith was bought by Messrs Spinks for £480 at auction sale held by Sotheby's, of London (see *Hull Daily Mail* 24 June 1971).

The Board of Trade file dealing with the awards is preserved in the Public Record Office, ref. MT9/769. Costello who was in Ireland at the time of the investiture, received his medal at the Board of Trade, 15 May 1905. (See P.E. Abbott and J.M.A. Tamplin *British Gallantry Awards*, pp. 22-23) .

Albert Medal; bronze, second class, awarded to Edwin Costello, bosun of the trawler Gull.

Edwin Costello as a young boy; the only known photograph.

Souvenir china figures of the fishermen's memorial; that on the left bears the mark of Swan china. (Chris Ketchell collection.)

THE GREAT
. RUSSIAN OUTRAGE . .

Perpetrated on Defenceless Fishermen, Oct. 21st, 1904.

ALL the world is amazed with horror and wonder,
At the Baltic fleet, that's made a great blunder;
Slaughtering with carnage the fishermen's lives;
Making homes desolate for children and wives.

Where was our Navy, with its boys of blue?
Permitting the Russians to slaughter and do
Men to their deaths, leaving fatherless sons.
Up boys, at 'em, and show them your guns.

Wipe these cursed Russians from off the blue sea,
Show them what's what, and who master can be,
Insulting humanity with bloodthirsty deeds—
Point your guns at 'em, and mow them like weeds.

Arouse, ye bulldogs, and sweep from the waves
These Russians of murder, and bloodthirsty knaves,
Don't let an insult be heaped on the name
That's noted for glory and the Navy's fame.

Show them the lion that within you lies,
Don't stand insults, and eat humble pies.
Mow them down with the cutlass so bright,
For all the world knows you are in the right.

Make them to know that Britons will not stand
Carnage and murder from anyone's hand;
Show these cursed Russians the laws of the wave,
Killing fishermen that the storms have to brave.

Remember the Trawlers and your men from Hull,
Get at 'em, boys, and down their flag pull;
Avenge the deeds of these bloodthirsty cattle;
Let 'em feel and hear the Lee-Enfield's rattle.

Don't waste a moment, but go straight ahead,
Catch the Russian raiders and plug them with lead.
Lion of strength, don't be clawed like a kitten,
Teased and mauled, and by the Russian bear bitten.

Just wag thy old tail with glory defiance,
For in thy great paws we place our reliance;
Don't purr and skit, with a playful bound,
Open wide thy jaws, let an angry roar sound.

Oh, lion of strength, don't stand like a sheep,
Remember thy sons in mourning do weep;
Friends that's been murdered by shot and shell.
Up boys, and at 'em, and send them to h——.

Thou majestic lion and king of the beasts,
Don't let the bear on thy harmless sons feast;
Show them the mercy our fishermen were given.
At them with fury, and don't be driven.

Can't you hear the widows' faint cry?
Up with your arms, to do or to die;
Don't let a deed of such murder stand over;
Down with the Russians, the plundering rovers.

Sons of England, from Thames to the Humber,
Lie awake with revenge and do not slumber;
Let these wilful butchers be now taught to feel
Humanity for others, or else the cold steel.

Let the nation all rise with one consent,
Make Russia to know and truly repent,
That England is England, and the lion must be
Master of the bear, and ruler of the sea.

H. BUTTERFIELD, 3, Castle Hill, Keighley.

A memorial poem written by H. Butterfield, Keighley, and apparently sold as a souvenir item.

9 The Opposing Fleets at Tsushima, 27-28 May 1905

	JAPANESE	RUSSIAN
Battleships		
First class	Mikasa (flagship)	Kniaz Suvorov (flagship) Sept. 1904 (sunk)
	Asahi	Borodino 1904 (sunk)
	Shikishima	Orel Oct. 1904 (captured)
Second class	Fuji	Osliabia 1901 (sunk)
Third class	Chin Yen	Navarin 1896 (sunk)
		Sissoi Veliky 1896 (sunk)
Cruisers and		
Armoured Cruisers	Nisshin	Dmitri Donskoi 1885 (sunk)
	Kasuga	Vladimir Monomakh 1885 (sunk)
	Azuma	Nakhimoff (sunk)
	Asama	
	Tokiwa	Izumrud 1904 (wrecked)
	Idzumo	Almaz (escaped)
	Yakumo	Aurora 1903 (captured)
	Iwate	Svietlana 1897 (sunk)
	Kasagi	Oleg 1902 (interned)
	Chitose	Jemtchug 1904 (interned)
	Niitaka	
	Otawa	
	Tsushima	
	Naniwa	
	Idzumi	
Coast Defence Ships etc.		Graf Apraksin (captured)
	Admiral	Admiral Ushakov 1895 (sunk)
	Nebogatov's	Admiral Seniavin 1896 (captured)
	Division	Nikolai I (flag)

As well as numerous torpedo boats, gunboats, and auxiliaries.
The captured Russian vessels *Seniavin* and *Apraksin* entered service in the Japanese Navy and were renamed the *Mishima* and *Okinoshima*.

This is a listing of the principal vessels involved in the action. The Second and Third Pacific Squadrons, according to Novikoff-Priboy, comprised 9 first class iron clads, 3 coast defence ironclads, 5 first-class cruisers, 3 second-class cruisers, 9 destroyers, 5 auxiliary cruisers, 4 transports, 2 tugboats and 2 hospital ships.

The Japanese fleet comprised 6 battleships, 8 cruisers, 16 light cruisers, 20 destroyers, 58 torpedo boats. Some 70% of these ships were foreign built, mostly in Britain.

In round figures Russian casualties were 5000 dead, 500 wounded and 6000 taken prisoner. The Japanese lost 600 men, dead and wounded.

The survivor

Remarkably, one vessel still survives which was present in the North Sea as part of Rozhestvensky's squadron, namely the cruiser *Aurora*. Launched at St. Petersburg, 11 May 1900, she survives as a reminder of the great historic events which overtook Russia in the twentieth century. She is 126.8m (416ft) long with a displacement of 6371 tonnes. Her armament included eight 6-in guns, twenty-four 75mm guns and eight 37mm cannon, as well as three torpedo tubes. At Tsushima, with a complement of 570 including 20 officers, she was commanded by Evgeny Yegoriev and he and nearly a hundred men were killed in the battle. On 25 October 1917 (old style) a blank shot fired from the forward gun while anchored off the Winter Palace in St Petersburg signalled the beginning of the October Revolution. From 1923 she was a sea-going training ship and was badly damaged during the siege of Leningrad (St Petersburg) when she was used as an anti-aircraft battery. After repair, *Aurora* became a naval training school, permanently moored at the Petrogradskaya Embankment. Here she still is, fully restored and open to visitors, with museum displays explaining her long history. She has the same resonance to the Russian people as the *Victory* to the British, and every year the graduation ceremony of future naval officers takes place on board.

The Russian cruiser Aurora; involved in the North Sea Incident, its forward gun signalled the start of the October Revolution, 1917. Photographed at her berth on the Neva, St. Petersburg.

As a gauge of public estimation of the contending powers, it is interesting to note that the Hull trawling firm of Pickering and Haldane, even before the North Sea Incident or TsuShima, departed from the traditional naming system of their vessels. Normally named after titled gentlemen, eg. *Lord Wolseley* etc, on 13 August 1903 the *Admiral Togo* was launched at the Beverley shipyard, followed the next day by the *Japan*. On the 5 June 1905 the *Mikado* was launched for Pickerings and in 1909, at Earle's shipyard, the *Yokohama*.

Links between Britain and Japan remained strong. The battleship Katori was launched at Vickers, Barrow-in-Furness by Prince Arisagawa, 4 July 1905

10 The Hull 'Box Fleet' c. 1870 - 1936

The type of fishing familiar to the modern generations of trawlermen involves working independently or 'single-boating'. For some seventy years the trawlers working out of Hull in the North Sea fishing grounds employed the fleeting system, a co-operative approach to fishing which had developed in the old sailing days.

It was an intensive, one might even say industrialised, form of fishing which maximised the catch and ensured the regular and speedy delivery of fish to market to supply the ever-growing demands of the expanding metropolis and industrial regions. Fleeting provided a lot of protein-rich food, cheaply, for the working man and was responsible for the burgeoning of that British institution, the fish-and-chip shop. Eventually to be found on almost every street corner, it was a reliable source of nourishing hot food and was vital to the livelihood of thousands of families. Poor housing conditions often made cooking difficult and the family routine usually centred around the breadwinners long working day of twelve hours, (more or less) which made regular meal times problematic.

Each trawler carried 120-160 tons of coal and stayed on the North Sea until it was used up. Large groups of vessels stayed at sea for several weeks at a time (8-12 weeks for the smacks, 5-7 weeks for the steam trawlers), transferring their catches to a fast cutter for rapid transit to market in Hull or London. Originally, the carrier boat was a fast sailing vessel, but these were replaced by steam cutters, which represent the first significant use of steam power on the fishing ground. The fleeting system was pioneered by the men of Kent and Essex, especially by the 'Short Blue' fleet of Hewetts of Barking, on the Thames. The latter moved to Yarmouth and at the time of the 'Russian Outrage' their fleet was laid up at Gorleston and the crews were seeking work elsewhere; Leggett killed aboard the *Crane* was from Gorleston.

Fleeting was introduced to Hull by John Sims (d. 1887), [32] principally because of the poor landing facilities given to individual smacks by the North Eastern Railway Company which controlled the docks. At this stage, bulk fleeting was the method employed, in which loose fish in baskets was taken off the smacks and put down between layers of ice in the fish hold of the cutter. Later the catch was transferred from trawler to carrier packed in boxes, each containing five or six stones of fish - hence referred to as the box or boxing system. Each loaded cutter would take some 1000 to 3000 boxes to the Billingsgate (London) market in a period of 30 to 36 hours.

The difficulties of shifting the boxes, first from the deck of the trawler down to the 16-feet rowing boat then up to the deck of the cutter, can easily be imagined.

John Sims, who introduced the Box or fleeting system to Hull c.1870.

The Great Northern Fleet under sail in the North Sea c.1880. The boats are tied up to the steam carrier vessel while unloading the boxes of fish.

On the deck of a Great Northern fishing smack c.1880. Using the steam winch (probably by Elliott and Garrood of Beccles, Suffolk) to bring aboard the trawl warp.

Transferring boxes between boat and trawler in the North Sea. Note the boxes are marked Kelsall, Bros and Beeching; c.1905.

Boats transferring boxes to fish carrier Columbia of the Great Northern Steam Fishing Co; built at Stockton-on-Tees 1886 by M. Pearson, sunk off Thornton Ridge 1 May 1915.

Zodiac; built at Earle's shipyard, Hull, 1882. Steam trawlers like this quickly superseded the sailing smacks in the Hull fleet.

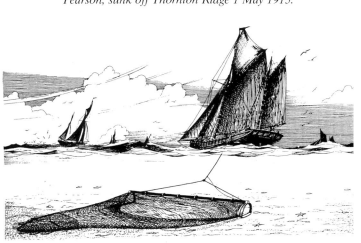

Method of fishing with a beam trawl.

Even a gentle swell made the operation hazardous and casualties were not infrequent. Weather in the North Sea can be horrendous and in the great storm of 1883 a total of forty-seven vessels and 260 men were lost on the evening of 6th March .[33] Most of the losses were on the Dogger Bank, where the set of the tide when confronted by a northerly gale results in a confused and dangerous sea. This and similar occurrences have been largely forgotten in the light of the attack by the Russian fleet in October 1904, which shocking as it was, resulted in only three men dead.

Many of the problems which arose on the North Sea were the result of being dependent on the vagaries of wind power. The arrival of steam meant that the vessel could fish even in a calm, could contend with difficult currents and more easily make a run for shelter if conditions were severe. Steam power first arrived on the fishing grounds with the replacement of the hand winch with a steam winch and the use of steam-powered cutters. The trawl could now be brought in without the need for massive physical effort by the crew, and the cutter (carrier) could reliably take its catch to market without fear of being becalmed.

Using paddle-tugs to hasten the passage out to the open sea led to experiments with tugs converted for fishing. These were tried with great success at South Shields and Scarborough and firmly established the idea of a steam-powered trawler. [34]   In 1881 Earle's shipyard in Hull launched the *Zodiac*, one of the first purpose-built trawlers. She was ordered by the Grimsby and North Sea Steam Trawling Co. [35] and carried a full set of sails, which not only helped economise on fuel consumption but provided propulsion if the engine failed. More than 160 vessels of this class were built and the yards of Cook, Welton and Gemmell and Cochrane's were quick to follow this example and established themselves as the two leading yards for construction of steam trawlers for Hull and Grimsby.

Although already in the 1870s smacksmen were complaining about declining catches, the introduction of steam for many years masked the reduction in fish stocks. A steam-powered trawler, towing at a predictable speed regardless of the actual strength of the wind, is obviously much more efficient than a sailing vessel dependent on a stiff breeze to reach the grounds quickly and tow its net to maximum effect.

The two largest outfits operating in the North Sea were those known as the Red Cross and Gamecock fleets, after the company symbols painted on their funnels, a St. George's flag and a red fighting cock respectively. The Red Cross fleet belonged to the Hull Steam Fishing and Ice Co., founded in 1876 when the Great Northern Fleet was also founded. In 1906 Hellyer's, who were already operating trawlers fishing independently at Iceland and the White Sea, also established a 'box fleet' and in 1911 had seven carriers and fifty-five fleeters operating in the North Sea. [36]

The demand for labour created by the box fleet drew in men seeking work from all over Britain and beyond. Walter Whelpton, skipper of the *Mino,* was from Gainsborough, Lincs, and his crew in December 1903 included S.B. Kemp, cook, also from Lincolnshire (Sleaford); Chief Engineer James Stubbs from Manchester; H. Ibbotson, deck hand from Bedford; F. Johnson, third hand, from Liverpool; W. Knight, trimmer, from Morpeth, Northumberland; and Hartfield the second hand from Stettin in the Baltic. The skipper received a 1 3/8 share of the profits, the second hand, a single share. Lower down the scale, the bosun was given 3d in the pound and a 20 shillings a week allotment for his wife. The third hand was given 2d in the pound and an 18 shillings allotment, and the deck hand and trimmer both received 16 shillings allotments, the former one penny in the pound as well. The chief engineer received 45 shillings and the second engineer 35 shillings. [37]

From 1921, though the vessels retained their separate liveries, the Gamecock and Red Cross fleets were run as a single enterprise. They continued in joint operation until forced into liquidation in 1936. This came about through a combination of rising coal prices, coal consumption by the fleeters was enormous - and intense competition from the 'single-boaters' fishing independently in the rich grounds off Iceland and Norway.

Kelsall's had their origins in Staffordshire (Skelton and Burslem), where they were fishmongers during the first half of the nineteenth century. A company called John Kelsall and Sons was founded in Manchester, 1850, and in 1876 they were owners of two paddle tugs in Liverpool. Possibly these vessels were being employed as trawlers. In 1892 Kelsall's had eight steam trawlers, which by 1896 had been transferred to Fleetwood, Lancashire, where development as a significant

fishing port had begun some five years prior to that.

The Beeching family had their origins in Kent (Bexhill, Ramsgate and Dover) and were mariners and shipowners, though in the merchant trade rather than fishing. James Beeching (1788-1858) established a shipyard c. 1860 at South Quay, Great Yarmouth, known in the 1870s as Beeching Bros. and built the *Sing Tai*, a bark for the China trade, the second biggest wooden vessel built at Yarmouth.

George Beeching appears in Hull in 1885 as owner and manager of the *Shoayayo*, a fishing smack, and by 1892 had five vessels registered at Fleetwood. 1897 saw the formation in Hull of Kelsall Bros. and Beeching, with John Kelsall, Thomas Kelsall, J.E.A. Kelsall and George Beeching as principals. The *Snipe* was the first fish carrier to be built for the new fleet and established the tradition of bird names [38]. A symbol of a red cockerel (hence Gamecock Fleet) on a white flag was the company's symbol which was painted on sheet metal applied to either side of the funnel of each vessel.

A painting of the s.t. *Ava* of Fleetwood (registration FD 145), built at North Shields in 1896 for George Beeching, shows a red funnel with a black top. On the mainmast is a plain blue pennant and on the mizzen a square white flag with a red gamecock. She was transferred to the Hull fleet in 1904 and was on the North Sea as part of the fleet which came under Russian attack. She foundered in the North Sea, 24 February 1910.

The vessels owned by Beeching's before the partnership was formed, typically had the names

Trawler of Hull Steam Fishing and Ice Co. (the Red Cross fleet); boat returning empty from the carrier.

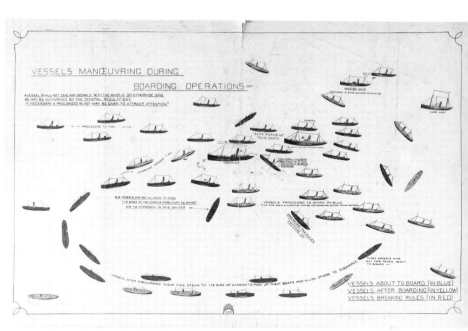

Plan of boarding operations for the Box Fleet in 1914; circulating anti-clockwise around the fish carrier.

Billingsgate, London; vessels of the Red Cross and Gamecock fleets alongside the quay with numerous tugs in the foreground.

Headed notepaper of Kelsall Brothers and Beeching, 1919.

John Kelsall (1835-1919), eldest son of Richard Kelsall (1803-1871).

75

of locations in Burma, many of which were still sailing at the time of the 'Outrage'. Kelsalls' vessels borrowed the names of P and O/White Star Liners, such as *Britannic* and *Majestic*.

During the day, the mark boat hoisted signals and indicated the assembly area for the fleet. The Admiral stood off from the carrier (cutter), whilst the trawlers circled in anticlockwise fashion, waiting for the signals for boarding to be hoisted at the foremast of the carrier.

Henry George Foot (born at Brixham 1844). Admiral of the Kelsall flee,t aboard s.t. Gamecock in 1905 with his dog 'Spot', a Jack Russell terrier.

Other signals were given by hand semaphore.[39] Small boats laden with full boxes rowed out to the carrier and returned empty to the parent trawler, which had in the meantime steamed to the lee side of the carrier. The whole operation took place under the constant direction of the Admiral, who employed signal flags by day and rockets and flares by night.

After the completion of the transfer, the trawlers returned to their fishing again; the Admiral's own vessel was fully employed catching fish when not in attendance on the fleet.

The Admiral, however, kept in touch with the other skippers as far as possible to prevent the fleet becoming too widely scattered and scouting trawlers would help direct them to the best fishing.

Before the 1914 war Walter Wood describes the scene as follows:[40] 'In ordinary circumstances a steam fleet of about 50 trawlers will be spread over an area of 7 or 8 miles. The mizzen is invariably set when trawling, and in some cases the mainsail as well. It is necessary when trawling to exercise great care, that the gear shall not be fouled'.

The fleet's operations are usually conducted within a radius of ten miles of the mark-boat. The method of discovering the fish and finding the shoals has been well described as 'skirmishing'. Each morning a carrier collects the fish and goes straight off to Billingsgate market (London), while another carrier, which has returned from the market, waits near the mark-boat in readiness to leave the fleet on the following morning. In ordinary circumstances there are two or three carriers with the fleet. The mark-boat may be called the rallying-point for the steam trawlers, which send their catches by the homeward-bound carrier and take empty boxes from the outward-bound carrier which has just joined the fleet after loading up at Gravesend with ice and coal.'

The routine continued day and night : 'The gear is shot about noon daily. By that time the men have boarded their fish and received their supplies of empty boxes from the carrier. For five or six hours the steamboats trawl at the rate of about two-and-a half miles an hour. A faster speed would mean the risk of damaging the gear and catching less fish. At about five o'clock in the afternoon the gear is hauled, and all hands are very busily employed in gutting and packing the fish. Meanwhile, the trawl has been shot again, and is towed until, at midnight, the admiral's signal to haul is seen and the gear is got up, to be shot again and hauled once more at about six o'clock in the morning. There are, consequently, three shoots and three hauls in the course of twenty-four hours'.

Wood gives us a description of the gear: 'The size of the net depends entirely on the power of the vessel using it; but the average size of a modern, North Sea otter trawl-net is about 100 ft. in length, with a spread of from 80 to 90ft. The otter trawling-boards are attached to the net, and it is the force of water passing between those boards which gives the 'spread' or, in other words, keeps the net open. The trawling warps are fastened to the boards, the length of warp used being regulated by the depth of water in which the vessel is fishing. Hundreds of fathoms of heavy wire warp are used by a steam-trawler, so that powerful steam-winches are necessary for hauling in the gear.

Trawl-nets are, or ought to be, high class Manila fibre, having great strength and being the best-known fibre for work in sea water. Otter trawl nets are generally coal-tarred, this tar acting as a preservative of the twine.'

The end of the Gamecock and Red Cross fleets came suddenly when the vessels were still at sea and the trawlers were taken into a variety of east coast ports and subsequently sold off:

Hull Daily Mail 6 March 1936

'End of two Hull Fishing Fleets-Shareholders agree to liquidation

'The shareholders of the Hull Steam Fishing and Ice Co. and of Messrs Kelsall Bros. and Beeching Ltd, today decided to put both companies into voluntary liquidation. Mr R F Helm of Messrs Hodgson, Harris and Co. being appointed liquidators. A committee of inspection also was appointed.

In a statement to the *Hull Daily Mail* it was revealed that approximately 800 men will be directly involved, and though the effect on them is regretted the shareholders are of the opinion that the fleeting system has become uneconomic and it is unwise to risk losing further money.

There is very little hope of selling the fleet as such, but there may be a chance that many of the boats can be converted and put into commission as single-boaters.

Meetings of the two companies were held at the Metropole, West Street, Hull, a meeting of the Hull Steam Fishing and Ice Co. being followed half an hour later by one of Kelsall Bros. and Beeching Ltd.

The share capital of Kelsall Bros. and Beeching is £74,000, the paid-up capital of the Hull Steam Fishing and Ice Co. Ltd. being £200,000.

In a statement to the *Mail* Mr H.F. Haywood, Chairman of the two companies, stated that both companies had been experiencing very heavy losses during the last few months owing to extraordinary weather conditions, and that in view of the rising price of commodities especially of coal - the directors felt that prospects of the companies were not sufficiently good to keep them going'.

The two companies, he said, have jointly consumed 100,000 tons of coal a year and during the last three years there has been an increase in the price of coal for trawler bunkers of 4s per ton. This item alone has meant there has been an increase in working expenses of about £20,000 a year. On the other hand the development of the now large, modern trawler has meant that fish can be caught very much cheaper by these new boats, which are fishing in very prolific fishing grounds in the White Sea, at Bear Island etc.

It generally has been considered that the fleeting system today has become an uneconomic one. Under these circumstances the directors and the creditors thought that the wisest course was not to risk losing further money but to put the companies into liquidation at the earliest date.

There are 60 ships in all involved and the firms employ about 800 men in Hull, in addition to the porters employed in the Billingsgate market.

The companies employ many men on the office staff and also salesmen who have been with us since they were boys, and the winding up of the companies falls very heavily on our servants of long standing.

The directors cannot see any other alternative although they have been making every effort to keep the company going.'

The present writer met and interviewed John Glanville Jnr (died aged 80 in 1987),[41] who served in the box fleet with his father John Glanville Snr (1881-1941), who was successively skipper of the *Esher, Evesham* and finally the *Solan*. The latter, and the *Grouse* (Charles Dixon, Vice Admiral) were the last two vessels built for the box fleet. His father, Tom Glanville, was a Devon fisherman and headed north in the middle of the nineteenth century at the same time the Hellyers left Brixham. The Silver Pits, with prolific stocks of sole, encouraged many fishermen to move north and exploit the northern waters of the North Sea.

Access to the industrial North and Midlands by railway from Hull, a link established in 1840, provided a ready market for fish and increasingly the fishermen of Brixham and Ramsgate began to settle in Hull to lay the foundations of a fishery which at the end of the century began to explore the distant water grounds off Iceland and Norway. Of Tom Glanville's two other sons, John and Ernest, both became trawlermen, the latter skipper of a 'single-boater' and Ernest a tug engineer.

John Glanville Snr. was born in Hull in 1881 and gained his skipper ticket on 8th June 1907 and thus firmly belongs to the era of steam-powered fishing. He joined Kelsall Bros. and Beeching as a young man and stayed with the company until its dissolution in 1936.

During the war he served in the RNR (T) and returned to fishing as one of Kelsall's most experienced skippers. From 1921 [42] he was a 'don' skipper, or Admiral, in charge of the manoeuvres by which the trawlers transferred their catches to the carrier boats. A plan, issued in 1914, clearly illustrates the congestion likely to result during this process and the probability of collision without the firm control of an able skipper who knew the nature of the fishing grounds intimately.

John Glanville Jnr. ,RNVR, M.B.E., was in the *Thanet* and *Buzzard* and left the 'box fleet' c. 1934, before it went into liquidation. He related that when the mark boat was anchored it remained so until the Admiral decided to move her and permanently showed a large flag on the foremast. Throughout his time he never saw semaphore flags in use; when he was bosun the latest news was passed from ship to ship in morse using a lamp, an occupation which helped pass the long morning watch.

Radio was installed on some of Hellyer's trawlers c. 1910 but was rare in the fishing fleet until after the 1914-1918 war. The cumbersome aerials were vulnerable to heavy weather and likely to be brought down.

Throughout the night the deck-hand on the Admiral's ship sent up a rocket on the hour and a flare on the half-hour.

When towing nets a red rocket indicated port side trawling and green that it was being hauled on the starboard.

Skipper John Glanville Snr (1881-1941) 'admiral' of the Box Fleet.

John Glanville Jnr (1907-1987).

Fish token Alf. Spring, fish merchant of Billingsgate.

Fish tokens; bottom, Hull Steam Fishing and Ice Co.

Fish token, Hull Steam Fishing and Ice Co (Red Cross fleet.)

Change of tack was also marked with rockets, red if going to port tack, green if starboard. Rockets were launched from holes in the rail set off by a red hot poker kept in the galley and hand flares were held out of the bridge window.

In a fog a 'gun rocket' (probably from a Very pistol or possibly a Schermuly rocket pistol) was sent up and this exploded with a loud bang. The boat carrying the full boxes was usually handled by the bosun and third mate and she was tied up with a four-inch 'grass' rope to a wire running by the side rail of the cutter. Wooden tallies with the name of the trawler were put in the boxes and up to 50 boxes of cod might be carried in one journey.

They were packed on two stages in the hold of the cutter (carrier), with broken ice scattered over the top.

No example of the wooden tallies has been seen by the present writer, but a variety of metal tokens or tallies bearing the name of the Hull Steam Fishing and Ice Co. are illustrated here.

A particularly decorative example in the form of a plaice has a stud on the underside and a dimple on the upper surface indicating that it was intended to be stacked. These tokens were possibly used on shore at market rather than on board ship.

A quarter scale model of a fish-carrying boat made c. 1883 is in the collection of the Hull Maritime Museum . Under the bow and stern sheets are galvanised iron air-tanks to ensure buoyancy even if swamped, and two small tanks of oil are placed aft for use in rough weather to calm the sea astern and prevent it breaking into the boat. A line is secured along the keel on each side, to which the crew can cling in case the boat should capsize. The craft required two men to manage them and had a carrying capacity of about two tons.

The drawing reproduced here was made by Mr W. A. Wriglesworth, who made many such boats c. 1920-30 as a shipwright on St Andrew's Dock.

An apprentice working at a firm employing the fleeting system spent three-quarters of his time in the boat shop, and only in the last month of his time was allowed to build his first boat.

They were not made to a plan or drawing but by eye, using the knowledge passed from one generation of craftsmen to the next. The strakes, thirteen on each side, were bent and shaped as the builder required while hot from the steam box. Typical dimensions were: length 17 feet, breadth 7 feet and depth 3 feet. They were rowed by two men, one facing the bow and

pushing and one facing the stern and pulling. In this way a heavy load was accommodated amidships and under the thwarts, whilst enabling an all-round watch to be kept on the seas from all quarters. The heavy swell and difficult cross-currents made life hazardous and boats were often overturned.

An account of the North Sea Fishery in 1883 concludes this section. This was a crucial period, the climax of the era of the traditional sailing smack but a time when fishermen were already reporting declining catches. Steam eventually replaced sail throughout Britain, but in Hull the transition was especially fast. By the 1890s most of the sailing smacks had been sold to other British fishing ports or abroad, especially to Scandinavia, Iceland and the Faroes. The use of steam and of the improved Granton trawl increased the catching power and masked the reduction of fish stocks.

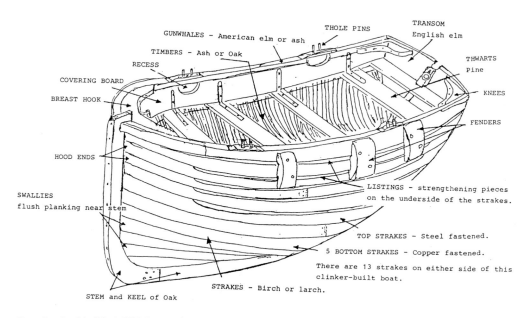

Drawing by Mr W. A. Wriglesworth.

NORTH SEA INCIDENT

Ketch or 'dandy-rigged' Regalia (H1490), c. 1885. The beam trawl can be seen lashed to the port side, an 'iron' at either end ran along the sea-bed lifting the net clear of obstructions.

True smack-rigged fishing vessel, the Barton Stather (H583) of Hull; 1865 a painting by C. Richardson.

This decline, combined with rising costs, finished off the box fleet in 1936 after a brief recovery of stocks when access to the North Sea was restricted during the 1914-1918 war. Similarly, the 1939-1945 war effectively created a moratorium on North Sea fishing owing to the danger of mines and attack by aircraft, submarines and surface ships. Sadly. the overfishing has continued and now all the important food fish species around our coast are under severe pressure.

Extracts from the *HULL WEEKLY EXPRESS* 15th September, 1883:

'At one time, when our vessels used to fish about the Botney, about September and

October, they found dogfish in immense numbers - as much as a ton at a haul would be got , but these have diminished very considerably. As they were full of herring when taken, it plainly indicated what work that had been on, so the herring fishermen have something to thank trawlers for, if they have the candour to admit it.[43]

Of the kind of fish which our trawlers now depend on for profit, the haddock and plaice are mostly sought after, as they are found in greater quantities - if there is a failure in the herring season, haddocks are of value for curing purposes, as they are bought instead of the bloater.[44]

Trawl fishing by day is not so profitable as at night. A day haul will not yield so much of the round fish - haddock, cod, ling etc. It may be assumed that the haddocks and cod rise from the ground by day and sink again at night, when they are caught in greater abundance. S and

82

SW winds are the best for fishing, with a nice moderate breeze, as the trawl is towed over the ground at a moderate rate and is kept open. N and NE winds are unfavourable, as the ground-swell caused thereby disturbs the fish.

Are trawl fish migratory? Doubtless, as fishermen know from experience, it is useless trying certain grounds in some months, but at regular periods fish will be found there, and they are pretty regular in the time of their return or taking off, as is the swallow. Our fishermen may be said to follow the fish, going from one ground to another as the seasons come round.[45]

The fishing grounds most frequented by vessels from the Humber are the shoal of the Dogger, the SW and NW spit of the Dogger, Clay Deeps, the NE part of the Dogger called the 'Cemetery' from the rough, stony nature of the bottom compared to gravestones, the Fisher Bank and beyond the Fisher Bank, Jutland Reefs, the Long Forties, the Horn Reefs, the Sylt and Amram Bank, Heligoland off the entrance to the Weser and Elbe, Nordney, Borkum, Terschelling, Texel etc., besides other grounds south of the Humber, such as the Wells Bank, etc. Messrs Hewitt (the Barking fleet) now rarely go fishing below Heligoland, but keep about Borkum and Nordney in the summer, and the SE part of the Dogger and Botney in the winter.

Plaice are to be found only in the spring and fall on the shoal of the Dogger, and in the summer on the Horn Reef and Borkum. In the winter, below the Dogger and off the Flamborough Head.

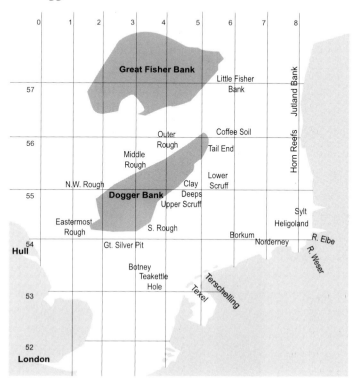

16998 **Billingsgate,**
HULL, ...193.....

To HULL ICE COMPANY, LIMITED.

Please deliver to bearer :—

.... *Kits Ground Ice*   *Stage*

....   "   "   "   *Town*

.... *Block Ice*   *(Loose)*

....   "   "   *(Packed)*

Received by :   **For P. M. PETERSON.**

Docket from the 1930s, for the supply of ice from Hull Ice Co.

Haddocks are to be found only in abundance on the SW spit of the Dogger, about October; in September they work along the pit edge of the Dogger and when taken, they are found to have plenty of herring and spawn in them.

Soles are caught on hard sandy ground, in warm weather taking the deep water, such as the pits, where the bottom is muddy and soft in winter, for warmth.

On the single-boating system a smack can remain away three or four weeks, icing and catching his voyage. A night haul is made by shooting the net about 8pm, trawling till three or four, about eight hours. A day haul is about five hours; but the length is necessarily regulated by the nature of the bottom where they are fishing. Under the boxing system the fish are sent to market every day by steam carriers, and the vessels fish in fleets together, and their movements are regulated under the control of an experienced fisherman, who is the appointed Admiral; these movements and also the fishing are controlled by means of the flag signals by day and by flares and rockets at night.

The steam cutter will bring to land from 1,000 to 3,000 boxes or trunks of fish containing 5 or 6 stones weight each, doing the distance in from 30 to 36 hours from fleet to port. After discharging cargo, she commences to load again with ice and empty trunks for the fleet at sea, taking out also clean clothing and many a loving epistle from dear ones at home, also stores of food and net, sails, rope, boats etc. Thus a continued communication is kept up with the land, and information supplied to those at sea, of all that is taking place on shore - the state of the markets, and so on.

Amongst these fleets may be seen the abominable 'coper' or floating grogshop doing its deadly work, but thanks to the Thames Mission, a powerful influence is now brought to bear against them by mission smacks, on board which the Bethel flag is hoisted and divine service held regularly on the Sabbath with excellent results. [46]

This system is pretty generally adopted in the summer months - from April to October - by the Hull and Grimsby boats. But there are some who still keep to the old bulk system of fleeting; these will join in companies of 20 to 30 boats, and share the result of the common catch at the end of the voyage - the duration of the voyage on the boxing and bulking system is about eight weeks. The difference is in the mode of conveying the fish to land and the

The City of Edinboro, built in Hull by William McCann in 1884. Here in dry dock under restoration; she was in sail again 1 April 1984, her centenary year. Now owned by Excelsior Trust, Lowestoft.

results. In the boxing system the fish is packed in boxes and ferried each morning to the steam cutter in attendance, is then put below and covered in ice, and soon the cutter is on her passage to Hull or London. In the bulking fleet, as it is termed, the fish is ferried to the sailing cutter, and then placed in alternative layers of ice and fish without boxes. On arrival at market the fish is picked by hand and filled in kits or turns, and sold in Hull, by weight, and Billingsgate, London, by package. When October comes a considerable number of boats leave the box fleet and the bulk fleets break up

partnership, and then resort to the single-boating system, by which each boat is on his own venture, and goes to what fishing grounds he fancies most. By taking in a stock of ice of from 5-8 tons, a vessel will continue on the fishing ground until he has secured sufficient to come with as a paying voyage. They will sometimes be away three or even four weeks, going so far as 240 miles or more from Spurn to the Fisher Bank and beyond, and fishing in 40 to 48 fathoms of water, These boats are mostly supplied with steam capstans and from 150 to 200 fathoms 7^{1}/$_{4}$ inch [47] trawl warp is required. The application of ice and steam to trawling has brought about wonderful change; by its aid the vessels have by degrees extended their searches after the finny tribe all over the North Sea, and there is not a patch of ground in it that is not as well-known to the experienced fisherman as the land on which we dwell, and in confidence he treads the deck as -

O'er the blue sea
His gallant barque bounds merrily
Bringing home to thousands of toiling creatures cheap and wholesome food'.[48]

The wooden fishing smack was a sturdy and versatile craft. In the Faroes many remained in use, fitted with a motor, for line-fishing. In September 1980, one of these Hull fishing smacks was brought back to the Humber by Dr. Henry Irving. He named her *William McCann* after the builder.

Originally the *City of Edinboro* (H.1394), she was built in 1884 for George Bowman and Richard Simpson, smack owners and fish merchants. After the rapid replacement of

NORTH SEA INCIDENT

sailing smacks by steam trawlers, this, like the rest of the local fleet, was put up for sale. She was bought by an Icelandic owner in 1897, then in 1913 transferred to the Faroes. With an engine installed in 1924 and the sail progressively reduced, she was employed in line-fishing up until 1980, a continuous working life of nearly a hundred years. Purchased by Dr. Irving, restoration to her original state progressed rapidly so that on the 1st April 1984, in her centenary year, she was able to make her first voyage under sail for sixty years.

Two months later the veteran Grimsby-built smack *Westward Ho* arrived on the Humber to challenge her to a race under sail along the east coast to Newcastle. Sadly the wind conditions were not helpful and both progressed most of the way using their engines. The *Westward Ho* based at Torshavn in the Faroes is owned and maintained by the local fishermen.

Though a number of the old sailing trawlers have survived there is only one North Sea steam trawler still in existence. This is the *Viola*, a vessel built for Hellyer's of Hull in 1906 at the Beverley shipyard. Sold abroad she was converted in 1922 for whaling off the African coast and then again changed owners to the Cia Argentina de Pesca in 1927 and in 1960 to Albion Star Ltd, registered at Port Stanley. Laid up in 1974, the whale-catcher *Pesca*, as she was renamed, still lies at her moorings in Grytviken, South Georgia. [49]

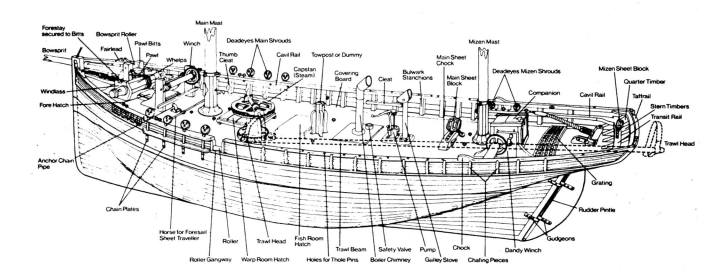

11 The Mission on the Fishing Grounds

In the days of sail, conditions on the North Sea fishing grounds were harsh; a tiny crew of five, usually three men and two apprentice boys, had to manage the sailing of the smack, manhandle the trawl net and the winch, as well as transfer the catch to carrier each morning. After about 1870 the old single-masted fishing smack, 50-60 feet long, was replaced with the two-masted ketch-rigged (often referred to as dandy-rigged) vessel of about 80 feet. To tow a net to maximum efficiency this large craft needed a stiff breeze to push it through the water or its catching power was severely reduced.

The effort of working a boat of this size, especially in the fleeting system, constantly attending the sails, steering by tiller, packing and transferring the catch, for weeks at a stretch, was all achieved by the five-man crew on a monotonous diet of fish and potatoes. The strain, both physically and mentally, can only be imagined, especially when one considers the often severe sea conditions whipped up in the shallow waters of the fishing grounds. Injuries and death were commonplace; the losses of 1883 were by no means unique, and in 1887 36 smacks were lost, 215 men and boys drowned; 1889, 94 fishermen were lost, nearly half of them from Grimsby; another 42 in 1890 and the same in 1891; and 146 men and boys in 1894, more than a hundred from Hull, who left 55 widows and 128 children.[50]

Many of the apprentices were from the workhouse or were sent to sea by a magistrate as an alternative to gaol. The tough conditions were often made even harder by the frequently brutal discipline meted out to these youngsters, who had to learn quickly or feel the rope's end, a fist or a boot. Sometimes the attacks were so ferocious and sustained that they can only be described as sadistic cruelty. In December 1881 William Papper, a cook apprentice aboard the Hull fishing smack *Rising Sun*, was subjected to frequent beatings, dowsing with freezing water and finally thrown overboard by the skipper, Osmond Otto Brand. When one of the crew turned 'King's evidence' Brand was brought to court, found guilty of murder and hanged at Armley gaol in Leeds, May 1882; William Marwood was the executioner.

A card showing William Papper and crew of the Rising Sun; circulated for sale as a souvenir.

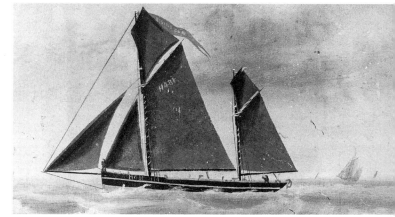

Smack Rising Sun (H481) owned and skippered by Osmond Otto Brand.

Dramatic scenes of the Box Fleet on the North Sea from the Mission magazine 'Toilers of the Deep'

Mission vessel Joseph and Sarah Miles in Hull after the North Sea Incident, 1904.

Skipper White of the Joseph and Sarah Miles at the time of the Russian Outrage.

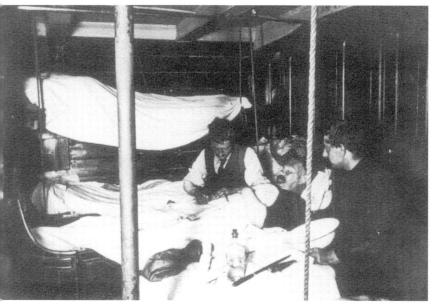

Sick berth; operation under way aboard a mission vessel c.1900.

The sick berth of the mission vessel Joseph and Sarah Miles, with the surgeon Hirjee Anklesaria and a portable X-ray machine.

This much-publicised incident, by no means unique, led to a debate about conditions in the North Sea fishing grounds and to better regulations by the Board of Trade. The *Rising Sun* was lost on 4 January 1883 when in the ownership of a Mr Biggins, the only man lost being Paul Lilley, a 16 year old apprentice; the rest of the crew were saved.

Such violent behaviour was often the result of drinking the cheap and 'poisonous' spirits sold by the Copers (properly Koopers, from the Dutch word for barter), who infested the North Sea. Cheap, duty free tobacco drew the fishermen to these 'grog boats' and they were tempted to buy large amounts of liquor as well as obscene prints and literature. In a drunken state - and lacking any more money - nets, rope and other gear, in extreme cases the smack itself, might be bartered for more liquor. Intoxication and lack of essential equipment in turn led to serious accidents and the loss of boats and men. The Copers were mostly based in Holland and Belgium but a few sailed from British ports.[51]

'One of these English craft was the *Annie*, sailing from the Humber, and others were the *Dora* and the *Angelina*, of Yarmouth. A man who served three years in the *Angelina* told him [the author] that they left Yarmouth with their gear aboard, like an ordinary trawler, and made straight for Nieudiep, in Holland, where they took in £500 worth of grog and tobacco. She then joined her fleet, and in one voyage alone the cargo would be sold and a profit made of 500 - 100 per cent., and that in two months. A bottle of rum was sold for 1s 6d, raw brandy at 2s, aniseed brandy - a dangerous and insidious spirit, and a great favourite with the smacksmen - 2s. 3d, and gin at 1s.

Such a profit as that - at the rate of 600 per cent yearly - was infinitely more than could be made out of the most successful trawling; but the system of copering, so far as English vessels were concerned, was not to become established or permanent. The danger was recognised in time and crushed out. The insurance clubs at home made it clear that these smacks were not wanted in the societies, there was opposition from one or two powerful owners, and there was always the peril of falling into the hands of the law and being severely dealt with. The English copers therefore ceased to ply their trade in the fleets, and one at least resumed her honest work of fishing.'

In the autumn of 1881 the idea was developing of providing help and support for the men and boys out in the North Sea. Ebenezer Mather [52] began the work of the Mission to Seamen (later the Royal National Mission to Deep Sea Fishermen, the royal prefix being granted by Queen Victoria in 1896), starting with the 56 ton yacht *Ensign* which left Yarmouth in 1882

Mission steamer Queen Alexandra with the Box Fleet.

In Memory of
WILLIAM PAPPER,
Who was Cruelly Murdered on Board the Fishing Smack "Rising
Sun," and his body thrown into the Sea Dec., 29th, 1881.

AGED 14 YEARS.

We cannot bend beside his grave
For he sleeps in the trackless sea
And not one little whispering word,
Will tell the place to me.

Memorial card for William Papper, aged 14 years.

after being altered to accommodate a missionary, creating a space for men who might want to go aboard and worship, as well as a dispensary equipped with a medicine chest. This and many other craft which followed were also working fishing smacks too and the catch helped to defray expenses. The fact that these were working boats and the early missioners were fishermen themselves quickly gained the respect and confidence of the smacksmen. The latter found both spiritual and practical support, cheap tobacco, extra provisions and rapidly improving medical help. [53]

'Two splendid craft, the *Queen Victoria* and the *Albert*, of 150 tons each, thoroughly well equipped in every way, and provided not only with a dispensary, but also with a hospital and accommodation for a resident doctor, because it was recognised that to be completely effective the vessels must carry a skilled surgeon to deal with the many accidents and ailments that are inseparable from North Sea Fishing.

There were ten berths in the large, airy hospital of the *Queen Victoria*, including two swing cots, most valuable in cases of fracture. The 'nurse' was a smacksman himself, and therefore one of the kindest and most willing of attendants on smacksmen who were sick or injured. The dispensary was excellently equipped, and a large number of out-patients could be attended with comfort at one and the same time.

The coper was fought with his own weapons, to a large extent. Tobacco was consigned to Ostend - 3 tons of it - and was put on board a Mission smack there, to escape the payment of duty. The smack went round the fleets, after leaving Ostend, and disposed of her 3 tons of tobacco at the actual cost price, 1s. per 1b, against the 1s 6d charged by the coper. Soon after this. the great firm of Messrs. W.D. & H.O. Wills offered to supply tobacco for sale in the fleets at approximately cost price, and they regularly sent large consignments of cut and cake tobacco, the cut in pound packets and the cake in 'pocket- pieces.

Owing to official aid and generous help from men of business, today (1911) on board any of the Mission vessels excellent cut tobacco can be purchased, duty free, at 1s 2d per lb, and cake tobacco at 10d, as against the coper's 1s. 6d and 1s and the smacksman is kept from temptation to drink, which was ever present on board the foreigner.

A Mission ship is one of the most interesting vessels afloat. She is a cruising hospital, a place of worship, a tobacco shop, a clothing establishment, a free library, a club room, a hotel and a recreation ground. If a smacksman is sick or injured, he will be fetched on board and receive skilled attention until he is better; if he wants to attend service and hoists a signal to indicate his wish, the Mission boat will call for him; tobacco he can obtain at cost price; warm woollen 'helmets', mufflers, stockings, and mittens he is able to buy for next to nothing; if he longs for something to read, he can have magazines and papers for the asking; if he has a craving to converse with fellow men, he can pace a clean attractive deck and almost forget the smell of fish. With the exception of the woollen articles - for which the Mission makes a small charge, as it has no intention of pauperising in any way - and the tobacco, everything is free, and there is plenty of it.'

The mission kept pace with modern developments, and as steam established itself on the fishing grounds they placed an order for a steam mission ship at a cost of about £12,000, paid for by an anonymous donor :

'This was the *Alpha*, built at Leith in 1900, a steel vessel of 275 gross tonnage and 70 horse-power. She was followed in 1902 by the *Queen Alexandra* and the *Joseph and Sarah Miles*, both built at Leith also, and provided with everything that can minister to the comfort and recreation of the men whose lives are spent on the North Sea. The three steamboats represent an original capital outlay of more than £34,000 and need a sum of £3,000 yearly - £1,000 each - to maintain them, although they are equipped with fishing gear and send their fish to market like the rest of the fleeters'.

Though no longer having a presence at sea the Royal National Mission to Deep Sea Fishermen still have missionaries at fishing ports throughout Britain, who offer practical and spiritual help to fishermen and their dependants.

Notes

1. All the contemporary local and national newspapers contain extensive reports of the North Sea incident as well as the progress of the Russo-Japanese war. The *Graphic* and *Illustrated London News* are filled with pictures and descriptions of the events of 1904-5.
   Richard Hough *The Fleet that had to die*, 1975, is the most accessible account of the progress of the Russian fleet to its final destruction at Tsushima.

2. The vessels involved were trawlers belonging to Kelsall Bros. and Beeching and James Leyman which were employed in the fleeting system.

3. *Hull Daily Mail*, Monday, 24 October, 1904 and *Hull Times*, 29 October, 1904, p.8.

4. There were in fact nine crew; he had not taken into account the cook, J.A. Smith, son of the skipper.

5. *Hull Daily Mail*, 24 October 1904.

6. *Hull Daily Mail*, 26 October 1904.

7. A copy of the typescript was given to the museum by Graham Paddison, in January 1983.

8. *Hull Daily Mail*, 28 October, 1904.

9. *Hull Daily Mail*, 31 October, 1904.

10. *Hull Daily Mail*, 27 October, 1904.

11. The hood of the foc'sle companionway of the *Mino* displayed in the Hull Maritime Museum, bears a brass plaque indicating that it was presented to the Chief Constable, Major Malcolm, by George Beeching in 1905.

12. See *The Fleet that had to die, The Tsars last armada*, and the contemporary newspapers and periodicals.

13. Fred T.Jane *Fighting Ships*, especially volumes for 1903-4 and 1905-6.

14. do.

15. The original manuscript is in the possession of Mrs Crockford, daughter of John Allan, now living in Queensland, Australia, who kindly supplied a photostat copy.

16. The 'Admiral' or 'don' skipper of considerable experience controlled the close manoeuvres of the fleet using flags, and rockets.

17. Hough *The Fleet that had to die*, p.67

18. do. p.68

19. *Hull Daily Mail*, 29 October, 1904.

20. *Hull Times*, 5 November, 1904, p.7. The coroner was Col. Thorney.

NORTH SEA INCIDENT

21. The action took place some miles east of the Dogger Bank, though the events are often loosely described under the title 'the Dogger bank incident'.

22. Copy in the Hull Local Studies Library; see also *Correspondence relating to the North Sea Incident,* February 1903 bound up in the same volume.

23. *North Sea Incident. International Commission of Inquiry: Despatch from the British Agent forwarding the Report of the Commissioners February* 1905 bound up with the Board of Trade Inquiry report and published Correspondence (see note 22 and bibliography)

24 *Hull Daily Mail,* 19 January, 1905.

25 See report of the Board of Trade Inquiry.

26 Walter Wood *North Sea fishers and fighters,* 1911. See chapter 22.

27 Camranh Bay (Vietnam) became the major Soviet naval centre on the Pacific coast, a warm-water base which allows warships to spend 75% more time at sea than is possible when stationed at Vladivostok.

28 *Hull Daily Mail,* 13 May, 1905.

29 He is buried alongside Smith and Leggett in the Hull Spring Bank cemetery.

30 See Jane's *Fighting Ships,* 1905-6.

31 *Hull Daily Mail,* 30 August, 1906. He was principal in the Wilson Line, which had long-established interests in the Baltic trade. C.H. Wilson also had a significant investment in the Red Cross fleet.

32 John Sims, at his death on the 21 April 1887, was chairman of the Hull Steam Fishing and Ice Co, and had for eighteen years been chairman of the Hull and Grimsby Mutual Insurance Society as well as chairman of the Hull Ice Co, Mast and Block Co, and the fund for fishermen's orphans.

33 These figures vary in the sources available and it seems that no definitive tally of casualties was ever made. See *Hull News,* Saturday, 24 March 1883, 'Hull smacks in the late gales'; and the *Daily Telegraph,* 23 April 1883 'A chat with a fisherman, by a seafarer'

34 Robb Robinson *Trawling* (1996)

35 J.W. Collins *Bulletin of the United States Fish Commission* (1890)

36 Walter Wood *North Sea Fishers and Fighters* (1911)

37 Hull City Archives. Fishing Crew Lists; DPF/24/729-730; DPF 21/887-888.

38 Most of the background information on the Kelsall and Beeching families was kindly provided by Mr N.A. Pearson.

39 Dyson (1977) p.103 records the signals used in the days of sail. See also a note in the *Mariners Mirror* vol. 10, no. 3, July 1924, p294.

40 This and the ensuing extracts are taken from Walter Wood (1911).

41 See obituary *Hull Daily Mail,* 16 June 1987

42 Credland (1985) *The boxing fleet: fishing log book 1920-1925 of Skipper John Glanville.*

43 More often the men of the herring drifters complained of their nets being torn by trawlers barging through them. Drift nets were suspended vertically in the water and were joined in series that could extend a distance of nearly two miles.

44 Bloaters were mildly smoked herrings unlike the 'red herring' and the kipper, which were given a longer cure and took on a deeper colouration.

45 The rise of the Hull trawling industry is associated with the discovery, in the middle of the nineteenth century, of the Silver Pits, a large depression south of the Dogger Bank which had a massive concentration of sole.

46 Devout Hull whaling masters in the Arctic fishery would sometimes carry a Bethel flag. All whaling activities were suspended on a Sunday and services held on board were open to the men of other vessels in the fleet.

47 Seven-and-a-quarter inches is the circumference of the trawl warp.

48 The industrial north and the densely populated capital provided a rich market for the fishermen of Hull and Grimsby.

49 See Robb Robinson and Ian Hart (2003)

50 Dyson (1977) p.159.

51 Walter Wood (1911).

52 Mather *Nor'ard of the Dogger* (1887).

53 Walter Wood (1911).

Bibliography

F.G. Aflalo *The Sea-fishing industry of England and Wales,* London 1904.

Anon. *The Listener* 24 March 1937, pp. 535-537. Eye-witness accounts of the North Sea Incident and its aftermath: (1) Thomas Carr (vice-admiral) of the Gamecock fleet, (2) James Hames, skipper of the Moulmein, (3) F. Houghton, preventive officer of customs (4) J.W. Tait, who collected much of the evidence for the Board of Trade inquiry.

Anon. editor (includes articles by Charles Hellyer and Christopher Pickering), *Hull as a fishing port,* Hull 1915.

Paul Barnes *The Mission Ships - the story of the Mission to Deep Sea Fishermen - afloat, 1882-1950* Gt. Yarmouth 1997.

George Blond *Admiral Togo,* London 1960.

J.W. Collins, 'Suggestions for the employment of improved types of vessels in the market fisheries, with notes on British fishing steamers' *Bulletin of the United States Fish Commission* vol. 8 (1888), Washington 1890. See section 2 pp. 183-188, for a detailed description of the *Zodiac.*

A.G. Credland *Iron and Steel Shipbuilding on the Humber;* Earle's of Hull, Hull Museums, 1982.

A.G. Credland *North Sea Incident, 21-22 October 1904;* commonly called the Russian Outrage (Malet Lambert Local History Originals nos. 33 and 34, Hull 1986.

A.G. Credland (ed.) *The Boxing Fleet; fishing log book 1920-1925 of Skipper John Glanville, Admiral of the Box Fleet in the North Sea* (Malet Lambert Local History Originals, vol. 27, Hull 1985.

Charles L. Cutting *Fish Saving - a history of fish processing from ancient to modern times* London, 1955.

John Dyson *Business in great waters,* London 1977

Susan Foreman *Loaves and fishes - an illustrated history of the Ministry of Agriculture, Fisheries and Food, 1889-1989* London 1989

Alec Gill *Lost Trawlers of Hull*, Hutton Press, Beverley, 1989.

Alec Gill and Gary Sargeant *A village within a city; the Hessle road fishing community of Hull,* Hull University 1986.

E.W.H. Holdsworth *Deep-sea fishing and fishing boats* London 1874.

Richard Hough *The fleet that had to die,* London 1958.

Fred T. Jane *The Imperial Russian Navy,* Portsmouth 1899.

Fred J. Jane *The Imperial Japanese Navy,* Portsmouth 1904.

Brian Lewis et al. *The day the Russian Imperial fleet fired on the Hull Trawlermen* - 1904.

(A peoples history of Yorkshire V), Hull Museums 1983.

Ebenezer J. Mather *Nor'ard of the Dogger,* London 1887.

A. Novikoff-Priboy *Tsushima,* London 1936.

Gordon Pearson *Hull and East Coast Fishing,* Hull Museums, 1976.

Constantine Pleshakov *The Tsars last armada - the epic journey to the battle of Tsushima,* London 2002.

Robb Robinson *Trawling - the rise and fall of the British Trawl fishery,* Exeter 1996.

Robb Robinson and Ian B. Hart 'Viola/Dias: the working life and contexts of the steam trawler/whaler and sealer,' *Mariner's Mirror* vol. 89 no. 3 (August 2003), pp. 325-338.

Yuri Shelayer, Elizabeth Shelayera and Nicholas Semenov *Nicholas Romanov 'Life and Death'* St. Petersburg, 1998.

David J. Starkey (editor) *England's Sea Fisheries - the Commercial Sea Fisheries of England and Wales since 1300,* London 2000.

Michael Thompson *Fish Dock - the story of St. Andrew's dock, Hull,* Hull 1989.

Michael Thompson, et.al. *Cook, Welton and Gemmell; shipbuilders of Hull and Beverley 1883-1963,* Hull 1999.

John K. Walton *Fish and chips and the British Working Class, 1870 - 1940,* Leicester 1992

E.W. White *British Fishing boats and coastal craft,* (Science Museum), London 1973.

T.J. M. Wood 'Sim's railway', *East Coast Digest* vol. 6. No. 3 June 1977, Sittingbourne, Kent. The introduction of the box system to Hull.

Walter Wood *North Sea fishers and fighters,* London 1911. The box fleet is covered in chapter X and chapter XVIII; the Mission in chapter XV and the Russian Outrage, chapter XXII.

See also the *Hull Daily Mail, Hull Times, The Times, The Daily Telegraph, Illustrated London News* and *The Graphic* especially vol. LXX, 29 October 1904 and supplement.

Preserved in the archives of Andrew M. Jackson, the firm of solicitors representing the trawler owners, is a copy of a comprehensive record of the evidence presented at the Board of Trade Inquiry. A paper bound volume of 315 pages it is entitled, *Board of Trade Inquiry into the circumstances connected with the North Sea Incident, 21-22 October, 1904; Minutes of Evidence* and *Appendix.* Also a brief printed document, 5 pages, entitled *North Sea Incident, International Commission of Inquiry. Statement of Facts submitted on behalf of His Britannic Majesty's Government,* London, 1905 as well as another copy of

Reports by the Board of Trade, as in the Hull local studies library collection and reprinted in the present volume (see note 23).

Also with Andrew M. Jackson are two foolscap scrapbooks with marbled boards; (a) 89 pages, titled in ink *Newspaper Cuttings re Russian Outrage*, and covering 24 Oct. 1904 to 31 Dec. 1904 (b) unnumbered pages, titled in ink North Sea Outrage Newspaper Cuttings, covering 20 Jan 1905 to 12 Nov 1906. The former includes illustrations from the *Daily Graphic*, 16, 17 and 19 Nov 1904 showing some of those present at the Board of Trade Inquiry held in Hull, and cuttings relating to attempts to bribe witnesses from the *Eastern Morning News, Standard, Daily Mail* and *Daily Chronicle*, 21 Dec 1904 and photographs from the *Illustrated Mail*, 23 Dec 1904, of Bennet and Walsh, two Englishmen alleged to be agents of the Russian government.

See also printed documents, entitled *Correspondence respecting the attack on Hull fishing-boats by the Baltic fleet, (October-December 1904)*, (232pp.) and *Further correspondence respecting the attack on Hull fishing -boats by the Baltic fleet (January to May 1905)* (312pp). Copies are to be found in the Admiralty library, Whitehall.

See also Hull City Record Office files TMM3/2/1-35; TMM3/2/2/1-166; and TMM3/2/3/1-99; which contain miscellaneous correspondence; letters of sympathy from all over Britain and overseas; offers of contributions to the relief fund, including proceeds of benefit performances at theatres in London and Fleetwood.

The North Sea Incident resulted in a flood of postcard photographs. These mostly show the damaged trawlers in the Hull fish dock, but also the funeral procession and the graves in the Western Cemetery and the fishermen's monument on the Hessle Road. Most of the cards have no indication of where or by whom they were produced, but there are some which form series and are furnished with a publishers name.

A numbered series was issued by Hickingbotham of Lincoln these have a white band on the right hand side which includes the publishers name and a description of the image which starts 'The Unwarranted Attack on British Steam Trawlers, in the North Sea, by Russian Gunboats during Friday night Oct. 21st 1904'.

Another numbered series was photographed in Hull by Turner and Drinkwater with the title 'British Trawlers Damaged by Russian Fleet' but published by Real Photo Series, Lankester and Co, Tunbridge Wells. Turner and Drinkwater also produced a series of official photographs of damage done to the trawlers, mounted on card (overall size 18¼ x 14in) which bear the stamp of the 'Medical Officer's Dept, Town Hall, Hull'.

A number of glass negatives of the victims of the 'Outrage' are preserved in the Hull Local Studies Library; presumably taken for the Hull coroner. An image of one of the crew, with the legend 'Trawlers fired on by Russian Warships Oct 21 - 04', is mounted on card, with the imprint of Parrish and Berry, Waltham St., Hull. James Stubbs, chief engineer of the *Mino* is posed at the entrance to the deckhousing.

Another numbered series has a title, in italics, 'Russian Outrage, Damaged Trawlers' etc, at the top left-hand side and Valentine Series, top right.